The Encyclopedia of Extraterrestrial Life

Annabelle Francis

BlueSky Art Publishing

Text © 2023 Annabelle Francis
Cover design and illustrations © 2023 BlueSky Art
Published by BlueSky Art Publishing
All rights reserved.
More information: www.blueskyart.nl

Contents

The Search for Extraterrestrial Life 9
    History of the Search 11
        Early Philosophical Ideas on Extraterrestrial Life 11
        Breakthroughs in Telescope Technology and Observations 12
        Pioneer and Voyager Missions' Contribution to the Search 13
    Methods and Technologies 14
        Radio Telescopes and SETI 14
        Space-based Observatories and Their Role 15
        Robotic Missions and Probes for Exploration 17
    Current and Future Initiatives 18
        Mars Rover Missions 18
        Europa Clipper Mission and Its Objectives 20
        James Webb Space Telescope and Its Potential Discoveries 21

The Origins of Life 23
    Theories and Hypotheses 25
        Primordial Soup Theory 25
        Panspermia Hypothesis 26
        Hydrothermal Vent Theory 27
    Extraterrestrial Conditions for Life 29
        Liquid Water and Its Importance 29
        Potential Energy Sources for Life 30
        The Role of Organic Compounds 32
    Astrobiology and Life's Requirements 33
        Habitable Zones and Planetary Factors 33
        Carbon-Based Life and Its Prevalence 35
        Extremophiles and Their Significance 36

Habitability in the Solar System 39

- Mars 41
  - Ancient Martian Environments and the Search for Fossils 41
  - Methane on Mars and Its Potential Biological Origins 42
  - Perchlorate Salts and Their Implications for Life 44
- Europa 45
  - Subsurface Ocean and Its Composition 45
  - Tidal Heating and Its Role in Maintaining a Liquid Ocean 47
  - Plumes and the Possibility of Sampling Ejected Material 48
- Enceladus 49
  - Geysers and Their Connection to Subsurface Oceans 49
  - Analyzing Plume Chemistry for Signs of Life 51
  - Future Missions to Investigate Enceladus 53

Exoplanets and the Goldilocks Zone 55
- Overview of Exoplanets 57
  - Detection Methods: Radial Velocity, Transit, and Microlensing 57
  - Types of Exoplanets: Super-Earths, Hot Jupiters, and More 58
  - Exoplanet Atmospheres and Biosignatures 60
- Habitable Zone and Factors 62
  - Defining the Goldilocks Zone and Its Limitations 62
  - Stellar Class and Its Influence on Habitable Zones 63
  - Planetary Factors: Size, Composition, and Orbit 64

Promising Exoplanets 66
- Proxima Centauri b and the Quest for Closest Habitable Exoplanet 66
- TRAPPIST-1 System and Its Multiple Potentially Habitable Planets 67
- Kepler-452b: Earth's "Cousin" and Its Similarities to Our Planet 68

Life Beyond Carbon 71
- Alternative Biochemistries 73
  - Silicon-Based Life and Its Theoretical Viability 73

- Arsenic-Based Life and Controversial Findings ... 74
- Non-Replicating Genetic Polymers as Potential Building Blocks ... 75
- Extreme Environments on Earth ... 77
  - Extremophiles in Acidic Environments ... 77
  - Life in High-Temperature Environments ... 78
  - Organisms Thriving in High-Pressure Conditions ... 80
- Implications for Extraterrestrial Life ... 81
  - Extremophiles as Analogues for Extraterrestrial Life ... 81
  - Constraints and Adaptations of Alternative Biochemistries ... 83
  - Prospects of Discovering Non-Carbon-Based Life in the Universe ... 84

Communication with Extraterrestrial Life ... 87
- The Search for Intelligent Extraterrestrial Civilizations (SETI) ... 89
  - History of SETI Initiatives ... 89
  - Radio Signal Detection and Analysis ... 90
  - Messaging and Active SETI Controversies ... 92
- Challenges of Interstellar Communication ... 93
  - Limitations of Light-Speed and Interstellar Distances ... 93
  - Communication Methods: Binary, Mathematical, Universal Constants ... 95
  - Technological Advancements and Future Possibilities ... 96
- Implications and Consequences of Contact ... 98
  - Cultural, Societal, and Philosophical Ramifications ... 98
  - Technological Impact on Humanity and Earth ... 99
  - Protocols and Ethics in Interactions with Extraterrestrial Life ... 101

Alien Abductions and UFO Phenomena ... 105
- Cultural and Psychological Aspects ... 107
  - Historical and Cultural Influences on Alien Abduction Claims ... 107
  - Psychosocial Explanations and Hypnotic Regression ... 108
  - Experiences and Narratives of Abductees ... 109

UFO Sightings and Encounters 111
Notable UFO Sightings 111
Military and Government Investigations 112
Analysis of UFO Evidence: Photos, Videos, and Radar Data 113
Critical Analysis and Explanations 115
Natural Phenomena Misidentified as UFOs 115
Psychological Explanations: Misperception and Illusions 116
Extraterrestrial Hypotheses vs. Skepticism and Debunking 117

Speculative Extraterrestrial Life Forms 121
Hypothetical Life Forms 123
Silicon-Based Life Forms and Their Characteristics 123
Gas Giants' Potential Floating Organisms 124
Bioengineered and Synthetic Life Forms 125
Alien Ecologies and Evolution 126
Adaptive Strategies in Extreme Environments 126
Exoplanet Ecosystems and Food Chains 128
Speculations on Alien Reproduction and Life Cycles 129
Creative Extrapolations 131
Science Fiction Depictions of Extraterrestrial Life 131
Imaginative Speculations and Alien Archetypes 132
Artistic Representations and Alien Aesthetics 134

Conclusion 137
Disclaimer 141

The Search for Extraterrestrial Life

History of the Search

Early Philosophical Ideas on Extraterrestrial Life

Ancient civilizations and early philosophers have long pondered the existence of extraterrestrial life, even before the development of modern scientific methods. Here are some notable early philosophical ideas on extraterrestrial life:

1. **Pre-Socratic Philosophers:**

    - **Thales of Miletus**: Proposed that water was the fundamental element from which all life arose, including potential extraterrestrial life.

    - **Anaximander**: Suggested the possibility of multiple worlds or universes, each potentially harboring life.

    - **Democritus**: Believed that an infinite number of worlds existed, each with its own forms of life.

2. **Epicurean and Atomist Philosophy:**

    - **Epicurus**: Argued that an infinite number of worlds exist in an infinite universe, and life likely exists elsewhere.

    - **Lucretius**: Elaborated on Epicurus' ideas, advocating for the diversity of life in the universe and the existence of extraterrestrial civilizations.

3. **Medieval and Renaissance Speculations:**

    - **Islamic Scholars**: Islamic astronomers and philosophers, such as Al-Farabi and Ibn al-Haytham, contemplated the existence of extraterrestrial life in their writings.

    - **Giordano Bruno**: Proposed the idea of an infinite universe with countless inhabited worlds, leading to his persecution by the Catholic Church.

4. **Enlightenment and the Copernican Revolution:**

    - **Nicolaus Copernicus**: The heliocentric model of the solar system challenged the notion of Earth's centrality, expanding the possibilities for life beyond our planet.

    - **Isaac Newton**: His laws of motion and universal gravitation provided a framework that supported the notion of a vast and diverse cosmos.

These early philosophical ideas laid the groundwork for subsequent scientific exploration and the search for extraterrestrial life. They sparked curiosity and set the stage for the development of technological advancements that would propel the search forward.

Breakthroughs in Telescope Technology and Observations

Advancements in telescope technology have been instrumental in expanding our understanding of the universe and driving the search for extraterrestrial life. Here are some notable breakthroughs in telescope technology and observations:

1. **Galileo's Telescope:**

    - In the early 17th century, Galileo Galilei revolutionized astronomical observations with his telescope.

    - Galileo made important discoveries, including the observation of Jupiter's moons, which challenged the notion of Earth as the center of all celestial motion.

2. **The Hubble Space Telescope:**

    - Launched in 1990, the Hubble Space Telescope has provided breathtaking images and valuable scientific data.

    - Hubble's observations have deepened our understanding of distant galaxies, star formation, and the age of the universe.

3. **Large Ground-Based Telescopes:**

    - Advances in ground-based telescopes, such as the Keck Observatory and the Very Large Telescope (VLT), have significantly improved our ability to observe and study celestial objects.

    - These telescopes employ techniques like adaptive optics, allowing for clearer images by compensating for atmospheric distortions.

4. **Radio Telescopes and SETI:**

    - The development of radio telescopes, such as the Arecibo Observatory and the Green Bank Telescope, enabled the search for extraterrestrial intelligence (SETI).

    - SETI uses radio waves to scan the cosmos for potential signals from advanced civilizations.

5. **Transiting Exoplanet Survey Satellite (TESS):**

    - Launched in 2018, TESS has revolutionized the field of exoplanet hunting.

    - TESS uses the transit method to detect small dips in brightness as planets pass in front of their host stars, identifying thousands of potential exoplanets.

6. **James Webb Space Telescope (JWST):**

    - Set to launch in 2021, the JWST promises to be the most powerful space telescope ever built.

    - It will observe in the infrared spectrum, providing unprecedented views of the early universe, exoplanets, and potential biosignatures.

These breakthroughs in telescope technology and observations have greatly expanded our knowledge of the cosmos. They have allowed us to explore distant planets, study the composition of atmospheres, and search for potential signs of extraterrestrial life. As telescope technology continues to advance, so too does our ability to unravel the mysteries of the universe and enhance the search for extraterrestrial life.

Pioneer and Voyager Missions' Contribution to the Search

The Pioneer and Voyager missions have played a crucial role in advancing our understanding of the solar system and expanding the search for extraterrestrial life. Here are the significant contributions of these missions:

1. **Pioneer Missions:**

    - Pioneer 10 (launched in 1972) and Pioneer 11 (launched in 1973) were the first spacecraft to travel through the asteroid belt and conduct close flybys of Jupiter and Saturn.

    - These missions provided valuable data on the gas giants' atmospheres, magnetic fields, and moons, increasing our knowledge of the outer solar system.

2. **Voyager Missions:**

    - Voyager 1 and Voyager 2, launched in 1977, embarked on an ambitious journey to explore the outer planets of the solar system.

    - Voyager 1 flew by Jupiter and Saturn, while Voyager 2 continued on to Uranus and Neptune, becoming the only spacecraft to visit these ice giants.

    - The Voyager missions revolutionized our understanding of these distant worlds, providing detailed images, atmospheric data, and insights into their moons and rings.

3. **Golden Record and Interstellar Messaging:**

    - Both Voyager spacecraft carried the Golden Record, a time capsule containing sounds, images, and greetings from Earth.

    - The Golden Record was intended to provide a snapshot of humanity and Earth to any potential extraterrestrial civilization that might encounter the spacecraft.

- While not specifically designed for communication with extraterrestrial life, the inclusion of the Golden Record symbolized our curiosity and desire to reach out to the unknown.

4. **Pioneering Interstellar Space:**

    - Voyager 1 and Voyager 2 have achieved remarkable milestones by entering interstellar space.
    - Voyager 1, in 2012, became the first human-made object to reach this vast expanse beyond the influence of the Sun, followed by Voyager 2 in 2018.
    - These spacecraft continue to transmit data back to Earth, offering valuable insights into the interstellar medium.

The Pioneer and Voyager missions have expanded our knowledge of the outer solar system, revealing the complexities and wonders of Jupiter, Saturn, Uranus, and Neptune. Additionally, through their interstellar trajectories and the inclusion of the Golden Record, these missions have symbolized humanity's exploration and potential contact with extraterrestrial life. The data collected and lessons learned from these missions have paved the way for future endeavors and inspired further exploration of the cosmos in the search for signs of life beyond our planet.

Methods and Technologies

Radio Telescopes and SETI

Radio telescopes and the Search for Extraterrestrial Intelligence (SETI) have been instrumental in the quest for detecting potential signals from advanced civilizations. Here's an overview of radio telescopes and their role in SETI:

1. **Radio Telescopes:**

    - Radio telescopes are specialized instruments designed to detect and study radio waves emitted by celestial objects.
    - They consist of large antennas and receivers capable of capturing faint radio signals from across the universe.
    - Radio telescopes can observe a wide range of frequencies, allowing for the study of various phenomena, including cosmic microwave background radiation, pulsars, and distant galaxies.

2. **SETI:**

    - The Search for Extraterrestrial Intelligence (SETI) is a scientific effort dedicated to detecting signals or evidence of intelligent extraterrestrial civilizations.
    - SETI researchers analyze radio signals for patterns or anomalies that may indicate artificial origin rather than natural phenomena.

- The primary approach is the analysis of narrowband signals at specific frequencies, which are less likely to be caused by natural sources.

3. **Breakthrough Listen and other SETI Projects:**

    - Breakthrough Listen, a prominent initiative in SETI research, was launched in 2015 with funding from the Breakthrough Initiatives program.

    - It employs state-of-the-art radio telescopes, such as the Green Bank Telescope and the Parkes Observatory, to conduct comprehensive surveys of the sky.

    - Breakthrough Listen combines advanced hardware and software technologies to analyze enormous amounts of data in search of potential signals.

4. **Signal Detection and Analysis:**

    - SETI researchers employ various methods to analyze radio signals, including spectroscopy, which examines the frequencies and intensities of received signals.

    - Efforts are made to distinguish between signals of terrestrial origin (such as human-made interference) and those that may originate from extraterrestrial civilizations.

    - Advanced algorithms and machine learning techniques are utilized to search for patterns and detect potential artificial signals within the vast amount of data collected.

5. **Messaging and Active SETI:**

    - Active SETI involves transmitting intentional signals from Earth to potentially habitable star systems, hoping to establish communication with extraterrestrial civilizations.

    - While controversial due to potential risks and ethical considerations, some projects have pursued active messaging, including the transmission of the Arecibo message in 1974 and subsequent transmissions by the Evpatoria Radar in Ukraine.

Radio telescopes and SETI techniques continue to evolve, driven by advancements in technology and our understanding of the universe. They offer a promising avenue to explore the possibility of intelligent life beyond Earth by listening for potential signals from distant civilizations and conducting active efforts to initiate communication.

Space-Based Observatories and Their Role

Space-based observatories have played a pivotal role in advancing our understanding of the universe and expanding the search for extraterrestrial life. Here's an exploration of the significance of space-based observatories in the quest for extraterrestrial life:

1. **Hubble Space Telescope:**
   - Launched in 1990, the Hubble Space Telescope (HST) has provided breathtaking images and valuable scientific data.
   - HST's location above Earth's atmosphere allows for clearer observations of distant objects, free from atmospheric distortion.
   - It has made significant contributions to the study of distant galaxies, star formation, and the identification of potential exoplanet candidates.

2. **Kepler Space Telescope:**
   - Launched in 2009, the Kepler Space Telescope revolutionized our understanding of exoplanets.
   - Kepler monitored the brightness of stars in a specific region of the sky, detecting tiny dips in brightness caused by planets transiting in front of their host stars.
   - Its observations led to the discovery of thousands of exoplanet candidates, including many in the habitable zone where liquid water could exist.

3. **Transiting Exoplanet Survey Satellite (TESS):**
   - Launched in 2018, TESS continues the work of Kepler by surveying the entire sky for exoplanets.
   - TESS uses the same transit method as Kepler but focuses on nearby and brighter stars, enabling more detailed follow-up observations.
   - It has already discovered numerous exoplanets, including some that are Earth-sized and potentially within the habitable zone.

4. **James Webb Space Telescope (JWST):**
   - Set to launch in 2021, the James Webb Space Telescope (JWST) promises to be the most powerful space telescope ever built.
   - JWST will operate primarily in the infrared spectrum, allowing for observations of distant galaxies, the early universe, and potential biosignatures on exoplanets.
   - Its advanced capabilities, such as the detection of atmospheric components, will contribute to the search for signs of life beyond Earth.

5. **Future Space Missions:**
   - Several upcoming space missions, such as the Wide Field Infrared Survey Telescope (WFIRST) and the European Space Agency's PLATO mission, will further advance our knowledge of exoplanets.

- These missions will characterize exoplanet atmospheres, study their habitability potential, and provide valuable data for future investigations into the existence of extraterrestrial life.

Space-based observatories offer unparalleled advantages for studying celestial objects, free from the constraints of Earth's atmosphere. They have contributed significantly to the discovery and characterization of exoplanets, expanding the possibilities for finding habitable environments and potential extraterrestrial life. With each new mission, our understanding of the universe and the search for life in the cosmos continues to deepen.

ROBOTIC MISSIONS AND PROBES FOR EXPLORATION

Robotic missions and probes have been critical in advancing our knowledge of the solar system and paving the way for potential discoveries related to extraterrestrial life. Here's an overview of the significance of robotic missions and probes in exploration:

1. **Mars Rovers:**
    - Robotic rovers, such as NASA's Mars rovers Spirit, Opportunity, and Curiosity, have greatly contributed to our understanding of Mars.
    - These rovers have explored the Martian surface, conducting experiments, analyzing soil and rock samples, and searching for signs of past or present life.
    - They have provided valuable insights into Mars' geological history, climate, and habitability potential.

2. **Cassini-Huygens Mission:**
    - The joint NASA-ESA Cassini-Huygens mission explored the Saturn system from 2004 to 2017.
    - The Cassini spacecraft studied Saturn and its moons, while the Huygens probe descended onto Saturn's moon, Titan.
    - The mission discovered methane lakes on Titan and revealed the potential for habitable environments beneath its icy crust.

3. **Voyager Interstellar Mission:**
    - The Voyager 1 and Voyager 2 spacecraft, launched in 1977, explored the outer planets and continue their journey into interstellar space.
    - These missions have provided detailed information about Jupiter, Saturn, Uranus, and Neptune, their moons, rings, and magnetic fields.
    - Voyager's ongoing transmission of data from interstellar space offers insights into the conditions beyond our solar system.

4. **Rosetta Mission:**
    - The European Space Agency's Rosetta mission (2004-2016) aimed to study Comet 67P/Churyumov-Gerasimenko.
    - The mission included a lander, Philae, which successfully landed on the comet's surface.
    - Rosetta provided crucial data on the composition of comets, offering insights into the role of these icy bodies in the origin of life on Earth.

5. **Future Missions:**
    - NASA's upcoming Mars 2020 mission will deliver the Perseverance rover to Mars, equipped with advanced instruments for astrobiology research.
    - The Europa Clipper mission by NASA aims to study Jupiter's moon, Europa, believed to have a subsurface ocean that could harbor life.
    - The Dragonfly mission by NASA will explore Saturn's moon, Titan, using a drone-like rotorcraft to investigate its organic chemistry and habitability.

Robotic missions and probes have expanded our knowledge of celestial bodies within our solar system and identified potential targets for further investigation regarding the existence of extraterrestrial life. These missions have revealed the geological, atmospheric, and chemical properties of various worlds, providing crucial insights into habitability and the conditions required for life. Continued robotic exploration will undoubtedly bring new discoveries and advance our understanding of the possibilities for extraterrestrial life.

Current and Future Initiatives

Mars Rover Missions

Mars rover missions have been at the forefront of the search for extraterrestrial life, with each mission building upon the discoveries of its predecessors. Here's an overview of notable Mars rover missions, including Curiosity and Perseverance:

1. **Curiosity Rover:**
    - NASA's Curiosity rover, part of the Mars Science Laboratory mission, landed on Mars in August 2012.
    - Curiosity's primary goal was to assess the past habitability potential of Mars by exploring its geology, climate, and the presence of organic molecules.
    - It has identified evidence of ancient Martian environments that could have supported microbial life, such as the discovery of organic compounds and the existence of a lakebed environment.

2. **Perseverance Rover:**
   - NASA's Perseverance rover, part of the Mars 2020 mission, landed on Mars in February 2021.
   - Perseverance builds upon Curiosity's achievements and aims to further explore Mars' habitability potential and search for signs of ancient microbial life.
   - It carries advanced scientific instruments, including a sample caching system to collect and store Martian rock samples for potential return to Earth in the future.

3. **Scientific Objectives:**
   - Mars rover missions focus on understanding Mars' past and present habitability, analyzing its geology, climate, and potential for hosting microbial life.
   - Key objectives include searching for biosignatures, assessing the distribution of water and organic compounds, and investigating the planet's geological history.

4. **Advanced Instruments:**
   - Rovers are equipped with a suite of advanced instruments to conduct their scientific investigations.
   - These instruments include cameras, spectrometers, drills, and sensors to analyze the composition, mineralogy, and atmospheric conditions of Mars.

5. **Sample Return Initiatives:**
   - Mars rover missions, such as Perseverance, are paving the way for future sample return missions.
   - The collection and return of Martian rock samples to Earth would allow for more detailed analysis, potentially revealing conclusive evidence of past or present extraterrestrial life.

6. **International Collaboration:**
   - Mars rover missions involve collaboration between international space agencies and scientists from various countries.
   - NASA's missions have welcomed contributions from international partners, such as the European Space Agency (ESA).

Mars rover missions represent significant milestones in our quest to understand the potential for life on Mars. With each mission, our knowledge of the Red Planet expands, and we get closer to unraveling the mysteries of its past habitability. The ongoing advancements in rover technology and the upcoming sample return missions hold tremendous promise for further exploration and the potential discovery of signs of extraterrestrial life on Mars.

EUROPA CLIPPER MISSION AND ITS OBJECTIVES

The Europa Clipper mission is a NASA-led endeavor aimed at exploring Jupiter's moon, Europa, and investigating its potential for habitability and the existence of extraterrestrial life. Here are the key objectives of the Europa Clipper mission:

1. **Study Europa's Subsurface Ocean:**

    - Europa is believed to have a global subsurface ocean of liquid water beneath its icy crust.

    - The mission aims to study the thickness, depth, and dynamics of this ocean to understand its potential habitability and the exchange of materials between the surface and the ocean.

2. **Characterize the Surface Composition:**

    - The Europa Clipper spacecraft will employ a suite of scientific instruments to analyze the composition of Europa's surface.

    - By mapping the distribution of different materials, including organic compounds and salts, scientists hope to gain insights into the moon's geological activity and potential for supporting life.

3. **Investigate Surface Geology and Icy Shell:**

    - The mission aims to map and study the various surface features of Europa, such as cracks, ridges, and impact craters.

    - By examining the surface geology and the characteristics of the icy shell, scientists can better understand the moon's history, tectonic activity, and the potential for material exchange between the subsurface ocean and the surface.

4. **Search for Plume Activity:**

    - Europa is known to exhibit occasional plumes of water vapor erupting from its surface.

    - The Europa Clipper mission will investigate these plumes and their composition, as they offer the opportunity to study the subsurface ocean and potentially sample it without landing on the moon.

5. **Assess Potential Habitability:**

    - The mission's primary objective is to assess the habitability of Europa by studying the moon's physical and chemical properties.

- Understanding the conditions necessary for life, such as the availability of energy sources, key elements, and the stability of the environment, will contribute to evaluating the potential for microbial life on Europa.

6. **Planetary Protection:**

    - The Europa Clipper mission also prioritizes planetary protection measures to prevent contamination and preserve the pristine conditions of Europa.
    - Strict cleanliness protocols are followed to minimize the chance of introducing Earthly microorganisms that could interfere with potential life forms on the moon.

The Europa Clipper mission represents a significant step towards unraveling the mysteries of Europa and assessing its potential for hosting extraterrestrial life. By exploring the moon's subsurface ocean, characterizing its surface, and investigating plume activity, the mission will provide critical data for future missions and enhance our understanding of the habitability of ocean worlds within our solar system.

James Webb Space Telescope and Its Potential Discoveries

The James Webb Space Telescope (JWST) is an upcoming space-based observatory that holds immense potential for expanding our knowledge of the universe and making significant discoveries related to extraterrestrial life. Here are some of the potential discoveries that the JWST may enable:

1. **Observing Exoplanet Atmospheres:**

    - The JWST is equipped with advanced instruments, including the Near-Infrared Spectrograph (NIRSpec) and the Mid-Infrared Instrument (MIRI), capable of studying the atmospheres of exoplanets.
    - By analyzing the starlight that passes through an exoplanet's atmosphere during a transit, the JWST can provide valuable insights into the composition, temperature, and potential signs of life-sustaining conditions.

2. **Characterizing Exoplanet Habitability:**

    - The JWST's observations will contribute to characterizing the habitability potential of exoplanets.
    - It can detect the presence of key molecules, such as water vapor, methane, and oxygen, which are important indicators of habitability and potential biosignatures.

3. **Studying Exoplanet Climate and Weather:**

    - With its unprecedented sensitivity and resolution, the JWST will enable detailed studies of exoplanet climate and weather patterns.

- By monitoring changes in the brightness and temperature of exoplanets over time, scientists can gain insights into their atmospheric dynamics and the potential presence of atmospheric phenomena relevant to habitability.

4. **Probing the Early Universe:**

    - The JWST's infrared capabilities allow it to observe distant galaxies and the early universe.
    - By studying the formation and evolution of galaxies, the JWST can shed light on the conditions that led to the emergence of life in the universe.

5. **Investigating Prebiotic Chemistry:**

    - The JWST's ability to observe organic molecules and complex carbon compounds in space will contribute to our understanding of prebiotic chemistry—the building blocks necessary for life.
    - By studying regions of active star formation, nebulae, and protoplanetary disks, the JWST can uncover the chemical processes that give rise to the conditions for life.

6. **Discovering New Worlds and Phenomena:**

    - The JWST's wide field of view and sensitivity will allow it to discover new exoplanets, including potentially habitable ones, and detect rare phenomena such as exomoons or planetary rings.
    - It will also contribute to the study of brown dwarfs, asteroids, comets, and other objects in our solar system, providing valuable insights into their compositions and characteristics.

The James Webb Space Telescope represents a major leap forward in our ability to explore the cosmos and investigate the potential for extraterrestrial life. With its advanced instruments and capabilities, the JWST has the potential to make groundbreaking discoveries, ranging from characterizing exoplanet atmospheres and habitability to studying the early universe and probing the chemistry of life. The mission will undoubtedly push the boundaries of our understanding and pave the way for future investigations into the existence of extraterrestrial life.

The Origins of Life

Theories and Hypotheses

Primordial Soup Theory

The Primordial Soup Theory, also known as the Oparin-Haldane hypothesis, is one of the prominent theories explaining the origin of life on Earth. It proposes that life emerged from a primordial soup of organic molecules in the early Earth's oceans. Here's an overview of the Primordial Soup Theory:

1. **Early Earth Conditions:**

    - According to this theory, around 4 billion years ago, the Earth's atmosphere was primarily composed of gases like methane, ammonia, water vapor, and hydrogen.

    - The absence of oxygen and the presence of intense energy sources, such as lightning and ultraviolet radiation, created an environment conducive to the formation of complex organic molecules.

2. **Organic Molecule Formation:**

    - Under these conditions, simple organic molecules, such as amino acids, nucleotides, sugars, and lipids, could have formed through chemical reactions.

    - These building blocks of life were likely synthesized in the Earth's oceans, as well as in hydrothermal vents and on the surfaces of minerals.

3. **Primordial Soup:**

    - The organic molecules produced from these reactions accumulated in the oceans, forming a "primordial soup" rich in complex organic compounds.

    - This soup was an ideal environment for chemical reactions and the subsequent formation of more complex molecules, including proteins, nucleic acids, and membranes.

4. **Prebiotic Chemistry:**

    - Within the primordial soup, these complex organic molecules could have undergone further chemical reactions, leading to the emergence of self-replicating molecules and early biological systems.

    - Over time, these systems became more efficient and complex, eventually giving rise to the first living organisms.

5. **Experimental Support:**

    - Laboratory experiments have provided support for the Primordial Soup Theory.

- In the 1950s, Stanley Miller and Harold Urey conducted the famous Miller-Urey experiment, simulating early Earth conditions and successfully producing amino acids, the building blocks of proteins.

6. **Limitations and Criticisms:**
    - Despite its significance, the Primordial Soup Theory has faced some criticisms and alternative hypotheses.
    - One criticism is that the early Earth's atmosphere might have been different than initially assumed, challenging the conditions necessary for the formation of organic molecules.
    - Other theories, such as the RNA World hypothesis, propose that self-replicating RNA molecules played a crucial role in the origin of life.

The Primordial Soup Theory remains a foundational concept in understanding the origins of life on Earth. While there are still unanswered questions and alternative hypotheses, the idea that life emerged from a rich mixture of organic compounds in the early Earth's oceans continues to shape our exploration and understanding of the fundamental processes that led to the existence of life.

Panspermia Hypothesis

The Panspermia hypothesis proposes that life on Earth may have originated from microorganisms or organic molecules that were transported through space from another celestial body. Here's an overview of the Panspermia hypothesis:

1. **Transfer of Life:**
    - Panspermia suggests that life's building blocks, such as bacteria, viruses, or organic molecules, could have been transported from one planetary system to another.
    - This transfer could occur through natural mechanisms like meteorite impacts, cometary collisions, or interstellar dust particles.

2. **Interstellar Panspermia:**
    - In interstellar panspermia, the hypothesis suggests that the transfer of life could have occurred between star systems within our galaxy.
    - It proposes that microorganisms or organic molecules could be shielded within comets, asteroids, or dust grains, and these objects could travel through space and eventually reach other planetary systems.

3. **Interplanetary Panspermia:**
    - Interplanetary panspermia focuses on the potential transfer of life within our own solar system.

- It suggests that life could have been transported from one planet or moon to another through impacts, where rocks ejected from a celestial body carrying microorganisms could land on another celestial body and potentially initiate life there.

4. **Potential Mechanisms:**

    - Various mechanisms have been proposed for the survival and transportation of microorganisms during panspermia.
    - These include the protection provided by the shielding effects of rocks or meteorites, the ability of microorganisms to withstand extreme conditions like radiation, freezing temperatures, or the vacuum of space, and the potential for dormant states or hibernation.

5. **Supporting Evidence:**

    - The Panspermia hypothesis finds some support from observations and experiments.
    - For example, microorganisms have been found to survive the harsh conditions of space during experiments conducted on the International Space Station (ISS).
    - Additionally, the discovery of hardy extremophiles on Earth that can survive in extreme environments raises the possibility of microbial survival during interplanetary or interstellar travel.

6. **Controversies and Challenges:**

    - The Panspermia hypothesis is not without its controversies and challenges.
    - Critics argue that the chances of survival and successful transfer of microorganisms over vast distances of space are extremely low.
    - Additionally, the hypothesis raises questions about the origin of life in the first place, as it does not explain the initial emergence of life on the donor celestial body.

The Panspermia hypothesis presents an intriguing perspective on the possibility of life's origins and the potential for its distribution throughout the cosmos. While it remains a subject of ongoing research and debate, further exploration and advances in astrobiology, space missions, and the study of extremophiles may provide valuable insights into the plausibility and implications of Panspermia in the search for extraterrestrial life.

Hydrothermal Vent Theory

The Hydrothermal Vent Theory proposes that life on Earth may have originated in the depths of the ocean near hydrothermal vents, where unique conditions fostered the emergence of early life forms. Here's an overview of the Hydrothermal Vent Theory:

1. **Hydrothermal Vent Environments:**
   - Hydrothermal vents are fissures in the Earth's ocean floor where heated water rich in minerals and chemicals is released from beneath the Earth's crust.
   - These environments are characterized by extreme conditions, including high temperatures, high pressure, and the presence of various inorganic compounds.

2. **Chemically-Rich Environments:**
   - Hydrothermal vents provide a rich source of chemical compounds, including hydrogen sulfide, methane, and metals, which can serve as energy and building blocks for life.
   - The mixing of hot, mineral-rich vent fluids with cold seawater creates a chemical gradient that could have provided the necessary energy and raw materials for the formation of organic molecules.

3. **Formation of Organic Molecules:**
   - The theory suggests that the interactions between the hydrothermal fluids and the surrounding seawater could have promoted the formation of complex organic molecules, such as amino acids and sugars, through various chemical reactions.
   - These organic molecules are the fundamental building blocks of life.

4. **Energy and Redox Reactions:**
   - Hydrothermal vents offer a unique combination of energy sources and redox reactions that could have fueled early life processes.
   - The chemical reactions between the vent fluids and the seawater create a range of energy gradients, such as those between hydrogen sulfide and oxygen, which could have provided energy for the synthesis of organic compounds and the sustenance of early life forms.

5. **Supportive Environments:**
   - Hydrothermal vent environments provide stable conditions, such as consistent temperatures and protection from external hazards like UV radiation and meteorite impacts.
   - These stable environments would have allowed for the accumulation and concentration of organic molecules and the formation of self-replicating molecular systems.

6. **Experimental Support:**

    - Laboratory experiments simulating hydrothermal vent conditions have shown that the synthesis of complex organic molecules and the formation of lipid membranes, similar to cell membranes, can occur.

    - Additionally, the discovery of diverse microbial communities thriving in hydrothermal vent ecosystems, often fueled by chemosynthesis, provides evidence for the potential of life in these environments.

The Hydrothermal Vent Theory offers a plausible explanation for the origins of life in extreme environments on Earth. It highlights the role of hydrothermal vents in providing the necessary energy, chemical building blocks, and stable conditions for the emergence of early life forms. Ongoing research and further exploration of hydrothermal vent ecosystems on Earth and potentially on other worlds provide opportunities to gain deeper insights into the potential for life beyond our planet.

Extraterrestrial Conditions for Life

Liquid Water and Its Importance

Liquid water is considered a crucial factor for the existence and potential development of life as we know it. Here's an exploration of the importance of liquid water in the context of extraterrestrial conditions for life:

1. **Universal Solvent:**

    - Water is often referred to as the "universal solvent" due to its unique ability to dissolve a wide range of substances.

    - This property enables chemical reactions necessary for life to occur, as dissolved compounds can interact and participate in biological processes.

2. **Solvent for Biochemistry:**

    - Within living organisms, water acts as a solvent for various biochemical reactions, facilitating the transport, interaction, and transformation of molecules.

    - Many essential biological molecules, such as proteins, nucleic acids, and carbohydrates, rely on water to maintain their structure and function.

3. **Temperature Regulation:**

    - Water exhibits a high specific heat capacity, meaning it can absorb and release large amounts of heat without significant temperature changes.

    - This property allows water to regulate temperature, buffering against extreme fluctuations and providing a stable environment for biological processes to occur.

4. **Facilitates Metabolism:**
    - Water is a vital component in metabolic processes, including enzymatic reactions and the breakdown and synthesis of molecules.
    - Many metabolic reactions within organisms require water as a medium and participate in maintaining homeostasis.

5. **Hydration and Biomolecules:**
    - Water plays a crucial role in the hydration of biomolecules, such as proteins and nucleic acids, contributing to their stability, folding, and functionality.
    - Hydration shells formed by water molecules around biomolecules ensure proper molecular interactions and enable structural integrity.

6. **Transport Medium:**
    - Water's unique properties, including cohesion, adhesion, and surface tension, enable it to act as a transport medium within organisms.
    - Water-based solutions, like blood in animals and sap in plants, facilitate the transportation of nutrients, gases, and waste products within the body.

7. **Potential for Life Support:**
    - Given the significance of liquid water for life on Earth, the presence of liquid water is often considered a key criterion for assessing the potential habitability of other celestial bodies.
    - The search for extraterrestrial life focuses on planets, moons, or other environments that may harbor liquid water, either on the surface or beneath the surface, as it provides a favorable environment for the emergence and sustenance of life.

Understanding the importance of liquid water in supporting life on Earth helps guide our exploration and evaluation of extraterrestrial environments for potential habitability. While the search for life beyond Earth encompasses a broader range of conditions and possibilities, the presence of liquid water remains a significant factor in assessing the potential for life as we currently understand it.

Potential Energy Sources for Life

Life, as we know it, requires a source of energy to sustain its metabolic processes and drive biological activities. While on Earth, energy is primarily derived from the Sun through photosynthesis, various potential energy sources could support life in extraterrestrial environments. Here are some examples of potential energy sources for life:

1. **Solar Energy:**
    - Sunlight provides abundant energy on Earth, driving photosynthesis in plants and powering the food chain.

- In extraterrestrial environments, such as planets orbiting within the habitable zone of their star, solar energy could be a potential energy source, supporting photosynthetic organisms and subsequent biological activity.

2. **Geothermal Energy:**

    - Geothermal energy arises from the heat generated within a planet or moon due to geological processes, such as radioactive decay or tidal forces.
    - Geothermal activity can manifest as hydrothermal vents, geysers, or volcanic activity, releasing heat and minerals into the environment.
    - In environments with geothermal activity, organisms can utilize this energy source for chemosynthesis, where they derive energy from the chemical reactions occurring in their surroundings.

3. **Chemical Energy:**

    - Chemical energy can be harnessed through various means, including the oxidation of organic or inorganic compounds.
    - In environments where organic matter is available, organisms can engage in respiration, breaking down organic compounds and using the released energy to drive biological processes.
    - Inorganic compounds like hydrogen sulfide, methane, or even metals can also serve as potential energy sources through chemosynthesis.

4. **Radiogenic Energy:**

    - Certain radioactive isotopes present in planetary bodies emit radiation as they decay.
    - Organisms capable of utilizing this radiation as an energy source, a process known as radiotrophy, could potentially exist in environments where radioactive isotopes are present.

5. **Tidal Energy:**

    - Tidal forces exerted by nearby celestial bodies can generate energy in environments with significant tidal activity.
    - On moons like Jupiter's Europa or Saturn's Enceladus, tidal forces due to gravitational interactions with their parent planet create tidal heating, which could provide a potential energy source for life.

6. **Electrochemical Energy:**

    - Electrochemical gradients, such as those created by the flow of ions across membranes, can be utilized as an energy source by certain organisms.

- In environments with significant ion concentration gradients, such as hydrothermal vents or brine pools, electrochemical energy can support the metabolic processes of specialized organisms.

It is important to note that the suitability and availability of these energy sources for supporting life depend on various factors, including environmental conditions, chemical composition, and the presence of appropriate organisms capable of harnessing and utilizing these energy sources.

Exploring and understanding the potential energy sources for life in different extraterrestrial environments expands our knowledge of the diversity of life-sustaining mechanisms and provides insights into the possibilities of life beyond Earth.

The Role of Organic Compounds

Organic compounds play a vital role in the chemistry and potential development of life. These carbon-based molecules are essential building blocks for the formation of complex biological structures and the facilitation of biochemical processes. Here's an exploration of the role of organic compounds in the context of extraterrestrial conditions for life:

1. **Carbon as the Basis of Life:**
   - Carbon is a versatile element capable of forming stable bonds with other elements, including itself.
   - The unique properties of carbon allow for the creation of diverse and complex organic molecules, making it a fundamental element for life as we know it.

2. **Building Blocks of Biomolecules:**
   - Organic compounds serve as the building blocks for essential biomolecules, such as proteins, nucleic acids (DNA, RNA), carbohydrates, and lipids.
   - Proteins are composed of amino acids, nucleic acids consist of nucleotides, carbohydrates are formed by sugars, and lipids constitute the structural components of cell membranes.
   - These biomolecules provide the structural framework and carry out crucial functions within living organisms.

3. **Information Storage and Transfer:**
   - Nucleic acids, specifically DNA and RNA, are responsible for storing and transmitting genetic information.
   - The sequence of nucleotides in DNA carries the genetic instructions necessary for the development and functioning of living organisms.
   - RNA molecules play a vital role in protein synthesis and gene regulation.

4. **Metabolic Processes:**
    - Organic compounds participate in various metabolic processes within living organisms.
    - Enzymes, which are proteins, catalyze biochemical reactions and facilitate the breakdown of organic molecules to release energy or the synthesis of new molecules.
    - Organic compounds, such as glucose, serve as energy sources through cellular respiration, allowing organisms to extract energy for their vital functions.

5. **Molecular Diversity and Complexity:**
    - Organic compounds exhibit a vast array of structures, allowing for a broad range of chemical and biological diversity.
    - The structural diversity of organic molecules enables the formation of complex macromolecules and the regulation of intricate biological processes.

6. **Prebiotic Chemistry:**
    - Organic compounds also play a significant role in prebiotic chemistry, which explores the chemical reactions that may have led to the emergence of life.
    - Prebiotic synthesis experiments have shown that simple organic compounds, such as amino acids and sugars, can be generated under conditions simulating early Earth or extraterrestrial environments.

Understanding the role of organic compounds in the context of extraterrestrial conditions for life expands our knowledge of the potential for life beyond Earth. Investigating the presence and distribution of organic molecules in various environments, such as the detection of organic compounds on Mars or in the plumes of icy moons, enhances our understanding of the possibilities for life's origins and existence elsewhere in the universe.

ASTROBIOLOGY AND LIFE'S REQUIREMENTS

HABITABLE ZONES AND PLANETARY FACTORS

Astrobiology is the interdisciplinary field that explores the origin, evolution, and potential for life in the universe. In understanding the conditions necessary for life, the concept of habitable zones and various planetary factors play a crucial role. Here's an exploration of the relationship between habitable zones and planetary factors:

1. **Habitable Zones:**
    - Habitable zones, also known as Goldilocks zones, refer to the region around a star where conditions are suitable for the existence of liquid water on a planetary surface.

- The habitable zone is characterized by a range of distances from the star where a planet can maintain temperatures that allow liquid water to exist, neither too hot nor too cold for life as we know it.

2. **Stellar Factors:**

    - The habitable zone depends on several stellar factors, primarily the star's luminosity and temperature.
    - A star's luminosity determines the amount of energy it emits, influencing the position of its habitable zone.
    - The star's temperature affects the spectral energy distribution, determining the range of wavelengths at which the star emits radiation.

3. **Planetary Factors:**

    - Planetary factors also play a crucial role in determining habitability.
    - Distance from the star: A planet's location within the habitable zone depends on its distance from the star, as it affects the amount of energy received and the potential for liquid water.
    - Atmosphere: A planet's atmosphere influences its greenhouse effect, which can help regulate surface temperatures. The composition and stability of the atmosphere impact the retention of heat and the presence of essential gases for life.
    - Size and mass: A planet's size and mass affect its geological activity, which influences factors like volcanic activity, plate tectonics, and the generation of a magnetic field. These factors impact the planet's atmosphere, climate, and overall habitability.
    - Composition: The presence of essential elements and compounds, such as carbon, nitrogen, oxygen, and water, is crucial for the formation of organic molecules and the potential development of life.

4. **Planetary Habitability:**

    - Habitability extends beyond the narrow concept of the habitable zone and includes various factors, such as the planet's geology, atmospheric composition, magnetic field, and potential for liquid water.
    - Planetary bodies like moons, even if outside the traditional habitable zone, could still possess conditions suitable for life due to factors like tidal heating or subsurface oceans.

Understanding habitable zones and planetary factors allows scientists to identify and assess the potential habitability of exoplanets and other celestial bodies. By studying these factors, we gain insights into the conditions necessary for life and the possibilities for finding habitable environments beyond our own solar system. The search for habitable worlds and the exploration of their unique characteristics bring us closer to unraveling the mysteries of life in the universe.

Carbon-Based Life and Its Prevalence

Carbon-based life forms, also known as organic life, are the foundation of life as we know it on Earth. The prevalence of carbon-based life in the universe is a topic of great interest in astrobiology. Here's an exploration of carbon-based life and its potential prevalence:

1. **Carbon's Unique Properties:**

    - Carbon is a versatile element with unique properties that make it well-suited for the formation of complex organic molecules.

    - Carbon atoms can form stable covalent bonds with other carbon atoms, creating long chains and intricate three-dimensional structures.

    - The ability of carbon to bond with various other elements, such as hydrogen, oxygen, nitrogen, and phosphorus, allows for the diversity and complexity of organic compounds.

2. **Organic Chemistry on Earth:**

    - Life on Earth is primarily composed of carbon-based molecules, including proteins, nucleic acids, carbohydrates, and lipids.

    - The abundance and diversity of organic compounds on Earth suggest that carbon-based chemistry is highly favorable for the emergence and evolution of life.

3. **Carbon's Abundance in the Universe:**

    - Carbon is one of the most abundant elements in the universe, formed through stellar nucleosynthesis in the cores of stars and released through stellar processes like stellar winds and supernova explosions.

    - The prevalence of carbon in various astronomical environments, such as interstellar clouds and planetary systems, suggests that the building blocks for carbon-based life may be widespread.

4. **Alternative Biochemistries:**

    - While carbon-based life is the only form of life known on Earth, the possibility of alternative biochemistries is a subject of scientific inquiry.

    - Silicon, for example, has been proposed as an alternative to carbon due to its similar chemical properties and ability to form stable bonds.

    - However, carbon's unique properties, including its flexibility, stability, and the abundance of organic compounds, make it more favorable for supporting the complexity and diversity of life.

5. **Conditions for Life Beyond Carbon:**
    - While carbon-based life is currently the focus of astrobiological research, the exploration of non-carbon-based life is crucial to understanding the full spectrum of possibilities in the universe.
    - Other elements and compounds, such as sulfur, nitrogen, and phosphorus, may play essential roles in alternative biochemistries.
    - Investigating the conditions under which life could potentially arise and thrive using different elemental and chemical frameworks expands our understanding of the potential for diverse forms of life.

Determining the prevalence of carbon-based life in the universe remains a fascinating area of research. The abundance of carbon, its unique properties, and the success of organic chemistry on Earth suggest that carbon-based life may be common. However, the exploration of alternative biochemistries is essential to broaden our perspective and uncover the full range of possibilities for life in the cosmos.

Extremophiles and Their Significance

Extremophiles are organisms that thrive in extreme environments that were once thought to be inhospitable to life. Their discovery has expanded our understanding of the conditions that can support life and has significant implications for astrobiology. Here's an exploration of extremophiles and their significance:

1. **Definition and Diversity:**
    - Extremophiles are organisms adapted to survive and thrive in extreme conditions, such as high or low temperatures, acidic or alkaline environments, high pressure, high radiation, or extreme salinity.
    - They can be found in diverse habitats, including hot springs, deep-sea hydrothermal vents, polar regions, salt flats, acidic lakes, and even within rocks several kilometers below the Earth's surface.

2. **Biological Adaptations:**
    - Extremophiles possess unique biological adaptations that allow them to withstand extreme conditions.
    - They may have specialized enzymes and proteins that function optimally under extreme temperatures or pH levels.
    - Some extremophiles can repair DNA damage caused by high radiation levels or survive in environments with limited nutrient availability.

3. **Insights into Life's Limits:**
    - Extremophiles provide valuable insights into the limits of life and the conditions under which organisms can survive and reproduce.

- By studying extremophiles, scientists can understand the biochemical and physiological adaptations that enable life to exist in extreme environments.
- This knowledge has implications for understanding the potential habitability of other planets, moons, or celestial bodies with extreme conditions.

4. **Origins of Life:**

    - Extremophiles offer clues to the origins of life on Earth and the possibility of life emerging elsewhere in the universe.
    - The extreme environments where extremophiles thrive may resemble conditions present on early Earth or other planetary bodies.
    - Studying extremophiles helps us explore the resilience and adaptability of life, shedding light on the potential habitats for life beyond Earth.

5. **Astrobiological Significance:**

    - Extremophiles have implications for the search for extraterrestrial life.
    - Their existence suggests that life might be able to withstand harsh conditions on other planets, moons, or even in the subsurface of icy worlds.
    - By understanding how extremophiles survive and thrive, scientists can identify potential habitable environments and refine their search strategies for life beyond Earth.

6. **Biotechnological Applications:**

    - Extremophiles produce unique enzymes and metabolites that have commercial and biotechnological value.
    - These organisms and their enzymes are used in various industries, such as bioremediation, pharmaceuticals, and industrial processes requiring extreme conditions.
    - Extremophiles offer a wealth of opportunities for developing novel biotechnological applications and technologies.

The study of extremophiles has revolutionized our understanding of life's adaptability and the conditions that can support its existence. They provide insights into the boundaries of habitability and have implications for astrobiology, origins of life research, and biotechnology. Exploring extreme environments on Earth and beyond unveils the remarkable resilience and diversity of life in the universe.

Habitability in the Solar System

Mars
Ancient Martian Environments and the Search for Fossils

Mars, often referred to as the "Red Planet," has been a focal point of scientific exploration due to its potential for past or present habitability. The study of ancient Martian environments and the search for fossils provide valuable insights into the possibility of life on Mars. Here's an exploration of this topic:

1. **Mars' Early History:**

    - Mars is believed to have had a more hospitable environment in its early history, with a thicker atmosphere, flowing water, and a warmer climate.

    - Geological evidence suggests the presence of ancient rivers, lakes, and even an ocean on Mars billions of years ago.

    - Understanding these early conditions helps in determining the potential for habitability and the preservation of possible biosignatures.

2. **Habitability Indicators:**

    - Scientists search for habitability indicators, such as the presence of liquid water, energy sources, and the availability of essential elements and organic compounds.

    - The identification of minerals, such as clays and carbonates, indicates the past presence of water.

    - The detection of methane, an organic molecule, in Mars' atmosphere also raises intriguing possibilities for the existence of microbial life.

3. **Mars Rovers and Landers:**

    - Rovers and landers have been instrumental in exploring Mars' surface and studying its geological history.

    - Missions like NASA's Curiosity and Perseverance rovers have provided valuable data about Mars' ancient environments and the potential for habitability.

    - These missions have analyzed Martian rocks and sediments, identified organic molecules, and investigated the planet's geology to understand its past habitability.

4. **The Search for Fossils:**

    - One of the primary objectives of Martian exploration is the search for fossilized evidence of past microbial life.

    - Fossils could provide direct evidence of ancient life forms on Mars.

- Scientists analyze rock samples, sediment layers, and mineral formations for potential fossilized remains or signs of past biological activity.

5. **Astrobiology and Mars' Significance:**
    - Mars holds significant astrobiological importance as it provides a laboratory to study the potential for life beyond Earth.
    - Studying Mars' past habitability and the search for fossils helps us understand the conditions necessary for life and the potential for its emergence and evolution.
    - Mars serves as a testbed for future exploration and colonization missions and provides insights into the challenges and possibilities of sustaining human life on other planets.

While the search for fossilized evidence of ancient life on Mars is ongoing, the study of Mars' ancient environments and the search for fossils contribute to our understanding of the planet's habitability. The data collected by rovers and landers, coupled with ongoing and future missions, continues to shed light on Mars' potential for hosting life and informs future exploration endeavors. Mars remains a captivating destination in the search for extraterrestrial life and the understanding of habitability beyond Earth.

Methane on Mars and Its Potential Biological Origins

Methane, a simple organic molecule, has been detected in the Martian atmosphere, raising intriguing questions about its origin and potential connection to biological activity. Here's an exploration of methane on Mars and its potential biological origins:

1. **Methane Detection on Mars:**
    - Methane was first detected in the Martian atmosphere by Earth-based telescopes in the early 2000s and later confirmed by orbiters and rovers.
    - The presence of methane is significant because it is a volatile organic compound that can be produced by both biological and geological processes.

2. **Geological Sources of Methane:**
    - Methane can be generated through non-biological processes, such as serpentinization, volcanic activity, and reactions between water and certain minerals.
    - Geological sources like hydrothermal systems or subsurface reservoirs could release methane into the Martian atmosphere.

3. **Biological Origins Hypothesis:**
    - Methane can also be produced by biological activity, including the metabolic processes of certain microorganisms known as methanogens.

- Methanogens are anaerobic organisms that thrive in environments with limited oxygen, such as wetlands, swamps, and the digestive systems of animals on Earth.
- The possibility of microbial life on Mars has led to the hypothesis that the detected methane could be produced by similar microbial organisms.

4. **Seasonal Variations and Methane Plumes:**
    - Observations have revealed seasonal variations in methane concentrations on Mars, with higher levels detected during certain times of the year.
    - In addition, localized methane plumes have been observed, indicating potential point sources of methane emissions on the planet's surface.
    - These variations and plumes provide valuable clues for understanding the dynamics of methane production and release.

5. **Current Investigations and Future Missions:**
    - Scientists continue to investigate the origins of methane on Mars through ongoing missions like NASA's Mars Science Laboratory (Curiosity) and the upcoming European Space Agency's ExoMars rover.
    - These missions aim to analyze the composition of Martian rocks, study the geology of methane-rich regions, and search for additional evidence of biological activity.
    - Future missions, such as NASA's Mars Sample Return, will collect samples from Mars and bring them back to Earth for detailed analysis.

6. **Unanswered Questions:**
    - The presence of methane on Mars remains an active area of research, and its definitive origin is yet to be determined.
    - Further investigations, including in-situ measurements and sample return missions, will help unravel the mystery of Martian methane and provide insights into its potential biological or geological sources.

While the presence of methane on Mars does not conclusively prove the existence of life, it is an intriguing finding that warrants further investigation. Understanding the origin and behavior of methane on Mars is crucial for unraveling the planet's past and present habitability and the potential for biological activity. Continued exploration and advancements in scientific techniques will shed light on the complex interplay between Mars' geological processes and the possibility of life beyond Earth.

Perchlorate Salts and Their Implications for Life

Perchlorate salts, compounds containing the perchlorate ion (ClO4-), have been discovered on Mars and have important implications for the potential habitability of the planet. Here's an exploration of perchlorate salts and their significance for life:

1. **Discovery of Perchlorate Salts on Mars:**

    - Perchlorate salts were first detected on Mars by the Phoenix lander in 2008 and later confirmed by the Curiosity rover and the Mars Reconnaissance Orbiter.

    - These salts, primarily in the form of magnesium perchlorate and calcium perchlorate, have been found in Martian soil and ice samples.

2. **Properties and Stability:**

    - Perchlorate salts are highly hygroscopic, meaning they readily absorb water vapor from the atmosphere.

    - This property allows perchlorate salts to lower the freezing point of water, making it possible for liquid water to exist at lower temperatures on Mars.

    - Perchlorate salts can also provide a source of oxygen when heated, which could be important for future human exploration and colonization efforts.

3. **Potential Effects on Organisms:**

    - Perchlorate salts have both beneficial and potentially harmful effects on organisms.

    - Some microbes on Earth are known to utilize perchlorate as an energy source, enabling them to survive in harsh environments with limited resources.

    - However, high concentrations of perchlorate can be toxic to certain organisms, inhibiting their growth and metabolic processes.

4. **Implications for Liquid Water:**

    - The presence of perchlorate salts on Mars has significant implications for the potential existence of liquid water.

    - The hygroscopic nature of perchlorate salts can allow for the absorption of atmospheric water vapor, creating brines with lower freezing points and increasing the possibility of liquid water beneath the Martian surface.

    - These brines may serve as potential habitats for extremophilic microorganisms that have adapted to survive in salty and low-temperature environments.

5. **Experiments and Research:**
   - Scientists have conducted laboratory experiments to investigate the effects of perchlorate salts on various organisms and to better understand their potential interactions with Martian soil and water.
   - These studies aim to determine the tolerance limits of different organisms to perchlorate concentrations and shed light on the potential habitability of Mars.

6. **Future Exploration:**
   - Future Mars missions, including sample return missions, will provide opportunities to analyze Martian soil and ice samples in greater detail.
   - By studying the composition and distribution of perchlorate salts, scientists can gain further insights into their role in Mars' habitability and potential for supporting life.

Perchlorate salts on Mars offer both challenges and opportunities in the search for life and the potential habitability of the planet. Understanding the effects of perchlorate salts on organisms, their role in water availability, and their distribution across Martian environments will contribute to our understanding of the potential for life on Mars and guide future exploration endeavors.

Europa
Subsurface Ocean and Its Composition

Europa, one of Jupiter's moons, has long fascinated scientists due to its potential for harboring a subsurface ocean. The presence of this vast ocean beneath Europa's icy crust opens up exciting possibilities for the existence of life. Here's an exploration of Europa's subsurface ocean and its composition:

1. **Evidence for a Subsurface Ocean:**
   - Observations from spacecraft, such as the Galileo mission, have provided compelling evidence for the existence of a subsurface ocean on Europa.
   - The moon's icy crust displays complex geological features, including fractures, ridges, and chaotic terrains, suggesting a dynamic internal oceanic environment.

2. **Composition of the Subsurface Ocean:**
   - The composition of Europa's subsurface ocean remains a subject of ongoing scientific investigation.
   - It is believed to be a salty water ocean, similar to Earth's oceans, but with a higher concentration of salts due to the moon's geological processes.

- The presence of salts, such as magnesium sulfate and sodium chloride, has been inferred from observations of surface features and the analysis of plumes erupting from Europa's surface.

3. **Thickness and Depth of the Ocean:**

    - The exact thickness and depth of Europa's subsurface ocean are not yet known with certainty.

    - Estimates based on gravitational measurements and modeling suggest that the ocean could be tens of kilometers deep, possibly encompassing more than twice the volume of Earth's oceans.

4. **Energy Sources for the Ocean:**

    - The subsurface ocean of Europa may receive energy from various sources, including tidal forces generated by Jupiter's gravitational pull and potential geological activity within the moon.

    - Tidal heating leads to the generation of internal heat, maintaining the ocean in a liquid state and potentially creating hydrothermal vents, similar to those found on Earth's ocean floors.

5. **Chemical Interactions and Habitability:**

    - Europa's subsurface ocean is in contact with its rocky mantle and may undergo chemical interactions that are essential for the development and sustenance of life.

    - The exchange of dissolved minerals, organic molecules, and heat between the ocean and the rocky interior could create a chemically diverse and potentially habitable environment.

6. **Exploration of Europa:**

    - Future missions, such as NASA's Europa Clipper, aim to explore Europa more extensively.

    - These missions will study the moon's icy crust, investigate its subsurface ocean composition, search for signs of life, and assess the moon's potential for habitability.

Understanding the composition and properties of Europa's subsurface ocean is crucial for assessing its potential for supporting life. The exploration of this fascinating moon promises to provide valuable insights into the habitability of icy worlds and the potential for life beyond Earth. Continued scientific investigations and upcoming missions will help unravel the mysteries of Europa's subsurface ocean and bring us closer to understanding the potential for extraterrestrial life in our own solar system.

Tidal Heating and Its Role in Maintaining a Liquid Ocean

One of the key factors contributing to the presence of a liquid ocean beneath Europa's icy crust is tidal heating. Tidal forces generated by Jupiter's gravitational pull induce internal friction and heat within the moon, maintaining its subsurface ocean in a liquid state. Here's an exploration of tidal heating and its role in maintaining a liquid ocean on Europa:

1. **Tidal Forces and Orbital Resonance:**

    - Europa's elliptical orbit around Jupiter and the gravitational interactions between the moon, Jupiter, and other Jovian moons create tidal forces.

    - These tidal forces cause the moon's shape to change slightly, resulting in the generation of internal heat due to friction.

2. **Orbital Resonance with Other Moons:**

    - Europa is in a unique orbital resonance with two other Galilean moons, Io and Ganymede.

    - This resonance amplifies the tidal forces experienced by Europa, leading to even greater internal heating compared to what would be expected from Jupiter's gravity alone.

3. **Flexing and Deformation of the Icy Crust:**

    - As Europa orbits Jupiter, the tidal forces cause the moon's icy crust to flex and deform.

    - The flexing generates heat through the friction between ice layers and the movement of subsurface materials, contributing to the internal heating of Europa.

4. **Internal Heat Distribution:**

    - The heat generated by tidal forces is distributed throughout Europa's interior.

    - The energy produced is dissipated as heat within the moon's rocky mantle and is transferred to the subsurface ocean, helping to maintain it in a liquid state.

5. **Hydrothermal Activity and Chemical Processes:**

    - Tidal heating also plays a crucial role in creating hydrothermal activity within Europa's subsurface ocean.

    - The heated water interacts with the moon's rocky mantle, potentially creating hydrothermal vents that release mineral-rich fluids and provide energy sources and chemical gradients necessary for life.

6. **Influence on Surface Features:**
    - The internal heating and the resulting subsurface ocean have a direct impact on Europa's surface features.
    - The constant movement and shifting of the icy crust due to tidal heating give rise to fractures, ridges, and chaotic terrains observed on the moon's surface.

7. **Significance for Habitability:**
    - Tidal heating is of great significance for the potential habitability of Europa.
    - The energy provided by tidal heating, along with the presence of a liquid water ocean, the availability of organic compounds, and the potential for hydrothermal activity, make Europa an intriguing target for the search for life beyond Earth.

Studying the mechanisms and effects of tidal heating on Europa is essential for understanding the moon's potential for supporting life. Ongoing and future missions, such as NASA's Europa Clipper, will provide valuable insights into the extent of tidal heating, the dynamics of Europa's subsurface ocean, and the overall habitability of this intriguing icy moon. By unraveling the mysteries of tidal heating, scientists are getting closer to unlocking the secrets of Europa and the possibility of life in our own solar system.

Plumes and the Possibility of Sampling Ejected Material

Europa has captivated scientists with its mysterious plumes—jets of water vapor and icy particles erupting from its surface. These plumes offer a unique opportunity to potentially sample material from Europa's subsurface ocean without the need for complex drilling missions. Here's an exploration of plumes and the possibility of sampling ejected material from Europa:

1. **Discovery of Plumes:**
    - Observations made by the Hubble Space Telescope in 2012 revealed evidence of intermittent plumes erupting from Europa's surface.
    - Subsequent observations and follow-up studies have confirmed the existence of these plumes, providing valuable insights into the moon's subsurface ocean.

2. **Composition and Origins of Plumes:**
    - The plumes are primarily composed of water vapor, along with other volatile compounds such as molecular hydrogen, nitrogen, and potentially organic molecules.
    - It is believed that the plumes originate from the subsurface ocean, propelled through cracks or vents in the icy crust, and ejected into space.

3. **Height and Distribution:**
   - Europa's plumes have been observed to reach heights of up to several hundred kilometers above the moon's surface.
   - Their distribution appears to be localized, with specific regions on Europa exhibiting higher plume activity.

4. **Potential for Sample Collection:**
   - The discovery of plumes opens up the possibility of directly sampling the ejected material without the need for complex drilling missions.
   - Flybys of future spacecraft, such as NASA's Europa Clipper, could fly through or near the plumes, allowing instruments onboard to collect and analyze the plume particles.

5. **Analyzing Ejected Material:**
   - Analyzing the composition of the plume particles can provide valuable insights into the chemical and biological characteristics of Europa's subsurface ocean.
   - By studying the isotopic ratios, organic molecules, and potential biomarkers within the plume material, scientists can gain clues about the potential habitability and the existence of life beneath Europa's icy crust.

6. **Challenges and Future Missions:**
   - Sampling plumes poses several challenges, including the need for precise timing and coordination between spacecraft and plume activity.
   - Future missions dedicated to exploring Europa, such as the Europa Clipper and potential Europa lander missions, will aim to characterize the plumes in more detail and assess the feasibility of sample collection.

The discovery of plumes on Europa has revolutionized our understanding of the moon's potential for harboring life. The ability to potentially sample ejected material from the subsurface ocean through plume flybys provides a unique opportunity to study Europa's habitability and search for signs of life. Continued research and upcoming missions will further advance our knowledge of these intriguing plumes and their significance for the search for extraterrestrial life in our solar system.

Enceladus
Geysers and Their Connection to Subsurface Oceans

Enceladus, one of Saturn's moons, has astounded scientists with the discovery of geysers erupting from its surface. These geysers are closely connected to subsurface oceans and provide valuable insights into the moon's potential for harboring life. Here's an exploration of geysers on Enceladus and their connection to subsurface oceans:

1. **Discovery of Geysers:**
    - The geysers on Enceladus were first observed by the Cassini spacecraft during its mission around Saturn.
    - These geysers are located primarily in the south polar region of the moon and were found to emit plumes of water vapor, ice particles, and other volatile compounds.

2. **Subsurface Oceans:**
    - The presence of geysers on Enceladus suggests the existence of subsurface oceans beneath its icy crust.
    - The geysers are believed to originate from fractures in the icy surface, providing direct access to the subsurface oceans.

3. **Composition of Plumes:**
    - The plumes emitted by the geysers consist primarily of water vapor, along with other components such as nitrogen, methane, carbon dioxide, and organic molecules.
    - These compositions provide valuable clues about the chemistry and potential habitability of Enceladus' subsurface oceans.

4. **Eruption Mechanism:**
    - The geysers on Enceladus are driven by hydrothermal activity.
    - Heat generated by tidal forces exerted by Saturn and the moon's internal heating processes lead to the formation of liquid water and the eruption of geysers.

5. **Enceladus' Tiger Stripes:**
    - The geysers are closely associated with a series of prominent fractures known as "tiger stripes" on Enceladus' south pole.
    - The tiger stripes are regions of increased geological activity and are thought to be the main conduits for the eruption of the geysers.

6. **Analyzing the Plumes:**
    - The Cassini spacecraft conducted flybys through the plumes, allowing instruments to directly sample and analyze the ejected material.
    - Analysis of the plume particles provided insights into the ocean's composition, including the presence of salts, silica, and organic compounds.

7. **Potential for Life:**
    - The hydrothermal activity, presence of organic compounds, and liquid water environments within Enceladus' subsurface oceans make it an intriguing target for the search for life.
    - The geysers serve as a means for sampling and studying the ocean's composition and potential habitability.

8. **Future Exploration:**
    - Future missions, such as the planned Europa Clipper, may also include investigations of Enceladus to further study its geysers and subsurface oceans.
    - These missions will focus on characterizing the geysers' activity, understanding the ocean's chemistry, and assessing the moon's potential for supporting life.

The discovery of geysers on Enceladus has revolutionized our understanding of this moon's potential habitability. The eruption of these geysers provides direct access to the subsurface oceans, allowing scientists to study the composition and conditions that may be conducive to life. Continued exploration and upcoming missions will further advance our knowledge of Enceladus' geysers and their implications for the search for extraterrestrial life within our own solar system.

Analyzing Plume Chemistry for Signs of Life

The geysers on Enceladus, with their plumes of water vapor and ice particles, offer a unique opportunity to analyze the chemistry of the ejected material for signs of life. By studying the composition of the plumes, scientists can gain insights into the potential habitability and the presence of biological processes within Enceladus' subsurface oceans. Here's an exploration of analyzing plume chemistry for signs of life on Enceladus:

1. **Plume Sample Collection:**
    - The Cassini spacecraft conducted flybys through the plumes, allowing instruments onboard to directly sample and analyze the ejected material.
    - Sampling the plumes provides access to material from Enceladus' subsurface oceans, where signs of life may be present.

2. **Identifying Organic Compounds:**
    - One of the primary objectives of analyzing plume chemistry is the detection of organic compounds.
    - Organic compounds are the building blocks of life, and their presence in the plumes could indicate the existence of biological processes within Enceladus.

3. **Mass Spectrometry:**
   - Mass spectrometry is a technique used to identify and analyze the composition of molecules in a sample.
   - Instruments equipped with mass spectrometers can analyze the plume samples for the presence of organic molecules and other compounds that may be indicative of biological activity.

4. **Biomarker Detection:**
   - Biomarkers are specific molecules or signatures that provide evidence of past or present life.
   - Analyzing the plume chemistry aims to identify potential biomarkers, such as specific amino acids, nucleic acids, or complex organic molecules associated with life processes.

5. **Isotope Ratios:**
   - Isotope ratios can provide insights into the origin and history of the plume material.
   - Variations in stable isotopes of elements, such as carbon, nitrogen, and oxygen, can indicate biological processes or geophysical interactions within Enceladus' subsurface oceans.

6. **Salts and Minerals:**
   - Analyzing the plume chemistry also involves studying the presence of salts and minerals.
   - Certain minerals or salts can act as energy sources for microbial life or indicate specific geochemical processes occurring within the subsurface oceans.

7. **Laboratory Studies and Simulations:**
   - Plume samples collected by spacecraft can be further analyzed in laboratories on Earth, providing more detailed investigations.
   - Scientists can recreate Enceladus-like conditions in laboratory simulations to understand the chemical reactions and potential habitability of the moon's subsurface oceans.

8. **Implications for Life:**
   - The analysis of plume chemistry plays a crucial role in assessing the potential habitability of Enceladus and the possibility of life.

- Identifying organic compounds, biomarkers, and other signs of biological activity within the plume samples would strongly suggest the presence of life or favorable conditions for life within Enceladus' subsurface oceans.

Analyzing the chemistry of the plumes on Enceladus provides valuable insights into the moon's potential for supporting life. By detecting organic compounds, biomarkers, and studying the isotope ratios, scientists can gain a better understanding of the habitability and the existence of biological processes within Enceladus' subsurface oceans. Continued research, further sample analysis, and future missions will continue to advance our knowledge of Enceladus and the potential for extraterrestrial life within our own solar system.

Future Missions to Investigate Enceladus

The intriguing discoveries made on Enceladus have sparked great interest in planning future missions dedicated to further investigate this enigmatic moon of Saturn. These missions aim to deepen our understanding of Enceladus' geysers, subsurface oceans, and the potential for life. Here's an overview of some of the future missions planned to explore Enceladus:

1. **Enceladus Life Finder (ELF):**

    - ELF is a proposed mission concept by NASA that focuses specifically on the search for signs of life on Enceladus.
    - The mission aims to fly through the plumes and collect samples to analyze for the presence of organic compounds, biomarkers, and other indicators of biological activity.

2. **Europa Clipper:**

    - While primarily focused on Jupiter's moon Europa, the Europa Clipper mission by NASA will also conduct flybys of Enceladus to study its geysers and subsurface oceans.
    - The spacecraft will carry a suite of instruments capable of analyzing the composition, chemistry, and potential habitability of the plumes.

3. **Enceladus Life Signatures and Habitability (ELSAH):**

    - ELSAH is a proposed mission concept by the European Space Agency (ESA) that aims to explore the habitability of Enceladus and search for signs of life.
    - The mission would include a combination of flybys and lander missions to investigate the plumes, subsurface oceans, and the potential for microbial life.

4. **Enceladus Explorer (EnEx):**

    - EnEx is a mission concept proposed by a team of researchers that envisions an orbiter and a lander mission to Enceladus.

- The mission would study the plumes, perform in-depth analysis of the subsurface ocean, and explore the moon's habitability using advanced instrumentation.

5. **Enceladus Life Signatures Mission (ELiMiS):**
    - ELiMiS is another mission concept proposed by a team of scientists that focuses on studying the potential habitability of Enceladus.
    - The mission would involve a spacecraft equipped with advanced instruments to analyze the plumes, study the subsurface oceans, and search for signs of life.

These future missions aim to build upon the discoveries made by the Cassini mission and further unravel the mysteries of Enceladus. By studying the geysers, plumes, subsurface oceans, and the potential for life, these missions will contribute to our understanding of the moon's habitability and the possibilities for extraterrestrial life within our own solar system. As mission plans develop and technologies advance, the exploration of Enceladus is expected to provide exciting insights into the potential existence of life beyond Earth.

Exoplanets and the Goldilocks Zone

Overview of Exoplanets
Detection Methods: Radial Velocity, Transit, and Microlensing

The discovery of exoplanets, planets orbiting stars outside our solar system, has revolutionized our understanding of the universe and the potential for extraterrestrial life. Detecting these distant worlds involves various methods, each offering unique insights into their characteristics. Here, we explore the primary detection methods used for exoplanets: radial velocity, transit, and microlensing.

1. **Radial Velocity Method:**

    - The radial velocity method, also known as the Doppler method, detects exoplanets by observing the gravitational effect they have on their parent star.

    - As a planet orbits a star, the gravitational interaction causes both the star and the planet to orbit around their common center of mass.

    - This motion induces periodic shifts in the star's spectrum, leading to changes in its radial velocity, which can be measured using spectroscopic techniques.

2. **Transit Method:**

    - The transit method detects exoplanets by observing the periodic dimming of a star's light as a planet passes in front of it.

    - When a planet transits its host star, it blocks a small fraction of the star's light, resulting in a detectable decrease in the star's brightness.

    - By monitoring the light curve, the changes in brightness over time, scientists can determine the planet's size, orbital period, and other properties.

3. **Microlensing Method:**

    - The microlensing method utilizes the gravitational lensing effect to detect exoplanets.

    - When a foreground star, acting as a gravitational lens, passes in front of a background star, its gravity can magnify the background star's light, creating a temporary brightening.

    - If a planet orbits the lensing star, it can produce an additional distortion in the light curve, revealing the presence of the planet.

4. **Advantages and Limitations:**

    - The radial velocity method is particularly effective for detecting massive exoplanets and determining their minimum masses.

- The transit method is sensitive to the size and orbital characteristics of exoplanets and has enabled the discovery of thousands of exoplanets to date.

- The microlensing method is most sensitive to massive planets located at large distances from their host stars.

- Each method has its own observational requirements, limitations, and biases, which affect the types of exoplanets that can be detected.

5. **Complementary Nature:**

    - These detection methods are often used in combination to confirm and characterize exoplanets.

    - Follow-up observations using multiple methods help validate the presence of exoplanets, refine their properties, and gather a more comprehensive understanding of their nature.

6. **Technological Advancements:**

    - Ongoing advancements in observational technology, such as high-resolution spectrographs, space-based telescopes, and large-scale survey projects, have greatly enhanced our ability to detect and characterize exoplanets.

    - New techniques and future missions, like the upcoming James Webb Space Telescope, will further expand our knowledge of exoplanet populations and their potential for habitability.

The radial velocity, transit, and microlensing methods have played pivotal roles in the discovery and characterization of exoplanets. Through these detection methods, scientists have unveiled a diverse array of exoplanetary systems, providing insights into their sizes, orbital characteristics, and compositions. Continued advancements in observational techniques and future missions will undoubtedly unveil even more exoplanetary wonders, fueling our quest to understand the prevalence and diversity of worlds beyond our solar system.

Types of Exoplanets: Super-Earths, Hot Jupiters, and More

Exoplanets exhibit a remarkable diversity in their characteristics, ranging from rocky bodies to massive gas giants and everything in between. Here, we explore some of the common types of exoplanets that have been discovered:

1. **Super-Earths:**

    - Super-Earths are exoplanets with masses higher than Earth but lower than Neptune or Uranus.

    - They can have rocky compositions, similar to Earth, but with larger sizes and stronger gravitational forces.

- Super-Earths may possess atmospheres of various compositions, including hydrogen, helium, water vapor, or even thick envelopes of gases.

2. **Hot Jupiters:**

    - Hot Jupiters are gas giant exoplanets that orbit very close to their host stars.

    - They have masses similar to or greater than Jupiter but exhibit scorching surface temperatures due to their close proximity to the star.

    - Hot Jupiters often have highly elongated orbits and may experience strong tidal forces and intense stellar radiation.

3. **Mini-Neptunes:**

    - Mini-Neptunes are exoplanets with masses and sizes between those of Earth and Neptune.

    - They have rocky cores surrounded by thick atmospheres composed primarily of hydrogen and helium, similar to Neptune and Uranus in our solar system.

    - Mini-Neptunes may also contain significant amounts of water, methane, or other volatile compounds.

4. **Gas Giants:**

    - Gas giants are exoplanets that are predominantly composed of hydrogen and helium, similar to Jupiter and Saturn.

    - They can vary in size and mass, with some being significantly larger or more massive than Jupiter.

    - Gas giants may possess a variety of atmospheric compositions, including clouds, storms, and dynamic weather patterns.

5. **Terrestrial (Rocky) Planets:**

    - Terrestrial or rocky planets, like Earth, are solid exoplanets with surfaces composed mainly of rocky materials, such as silicates and metals.

    - They have relatively smaller sizes and masses compared to gas giants.

    - Terrestrial planets may have thin or dense atmospheres, and they are of particular interest when studying potential habitability and the presence of liquid water.

6. **Exoplanets in Habitable Zones:**
   - Habitable zones, also known as Goldilocks zones, are regions around a star where conditions may be favorable for the existence of liquid water on an exoplanet's surface.
   - Exoplanets within the habitable zones of their host stars are of significant interest in the search for potentially habitable environments and the existence of extraterrestrial life.

7. **Exoplanets with Unusual Characteristics:**
   - Some exoplanets exhibit unique characteristics that defy traditional categorizations.
   - These include rogue planets that wander through space without a parent star, tidally locked planets with one side perpetually facing their star, and even exoplanets in binary star systems.

The discovery of various types of exoplanets has expanded our understanding of planetary systems beyond our solar system. These diverse worlds offer valuable insights into the formation, composition, and evolution of planets. By studying their atmospheres, compositions, and habitability potential, scientists continue to unravel the mysteries of exoplanets and the possibilities for life beyond Earth.

Exoplanet Atmospheres and Biosignatures

The study of exoplanet atmospheres provides valuable information about their compositions, climates, and potential for hosting life. By analyzing the chemical makeup of exoplanet atmospheres, scientists can search for biosignatures, which are indicators of biological activity. Here, we delve into the fascinating world of exoplanet atmospheres and the search for biosignatures:

1. **Atmospheric Composition:**
   - Exoplanet atmospheres can be composed of various gases, including hydrogen, helium, water vapor, carbon dioxide, methane, and nitrogen.
   - The composition depends on factors such as the planet's formation, proximity to its host star, and the presence of geological or biological processes.

2. **Transmission Spectroscopy:**
   - Transmission spectroscopy is a technique used to study exoplanet atmospheres by observing the starlight that passes through the planet's atmosphere during a transit event.
   - By analyzing the absorption features in the transmitted light, scientists can infer the presence and abundance of different atmospheric components.

3. **Emission Spectroscopy:**

    - Emission spectroscopy involves studying the thermal radiation emitted by an exoplanet to characterize its atmosphere.
    - By measuring the infrared emission from an exoplanet, scientists can determine the temperature profile, detect specific molecules, and study their abundance.

4. **Biosignatures:**

    - Biosignatures are measurable features or combinations of gases that could indicate the presence of life on an exoplanet.
    - Some potential biosignatures include the simultaneous presence of oxygen and methane, which on Earth are primarily produced by life processes.
    - Other biosignatures could include the presence of certain organic molecules, such as certain volatile compounds or complex hydrocarbons.

5. **False Positives and False Negatives:**

    - Identifying biosignatures in exoplanet atmospheres is a complex task due to the possibility of false positives and false negatives.
    - False positives refer to cases where non-biological processes or atmospheric chemistry can produce similar signatures to those associated with life.
    - False negatives occur when certain biosignatures are absent or undetectable due to limitations in instrumentation or incomplete understanding of life's diversity.

6. **Future Missions and Instrumentation:**

    - Future missions, such as the James Webb Space Telescope and the proposed ARIEL mission, will greatly enhance our ability to study exoplanet atmospheres and search for biosignatures.
    - These missions will provide higher sensitivity, resolution, and wavelength coverage, enabling more detailed investigations of exoplanet atmospheres.

Studying exoplanet atmospheres and searching for biosignatures is a crucial step in the quest to identify potentially habitable worlds and detect signs of extraterrestrial life. Continued advancements in observational techniques, instrumentation, and data analysis methods will expand our knowledge of exoplanet atmospheres and increase the chances of discovering life beyond our solar system.

Habitable Zone and Factors

Defining the Goldilocks Zone and Its Limitations

The concept of the Goldilocks Zone, also known as the habitable zone, refers to the region around a star where conditions may be suitable for the existence of liquid water on the surface of an orbiting planet. However, defining the boundaries of the habitable zone and its limitations is a complex task that requires considering various factors:

1. **Definition of the Habitable Zone:**

    - The habitable zone is defined as the range of distances from a star where a planet could maintain liquid water on its surface, assuming certain atmospheric and geological conditions.

    - It is based on the understanding that liquid water is essential for life as we know it.

2. **Factors Affecting the Habitable Zone:**

    - The position of a planet within the habitable zone depends primarily on the star's luminosity, spectral type, and the planet's atmospheric properties.

    - A star's luminosity determines the distance at which a planet must orbit to receive sufficient energy for water to remain in liquid form.

    - The planet's atmospheric properties, such as greenhouse gases, influence its ability to regulate temperatures and retain liquid water.

3. **Limitations of the Habitable Zone Concept:**

    - The habitable zone concept assumes that liquid water is a key requirement for life, but it does not guarantee the presence of life itself.

    - The habitable zone is based on Earth's conditions and the assumption that life elsewhere may have similar requirements, which may not necessarily be the case.

    - Other factors, such as the planet's composition, geological activity, magnetic field, and atmospheric dynamics, also play crucial roles in a planet's habitability.

4. **Inner and Outer Edges of the Habitable Zone:**

    - The inner edge of the habitable zone is defined by the point at which a planet becomes too hot for liquid water to exist due to intense stellar radiation.

    - The outer edge of the habitable zone is determined by the point at which a planet becomes too cold for liquid water to be present on its surface.

5. **Variability within the Habitable Zone:**
    - The habitable zone is not a fixed, static region but can vary depending on different factors.
    - Factors such as the planet's atmospheric composition, cloud cover, and the presence of feedback mechanisms can influence the habitability of a planet within the zone.

6. **Beyond the Habitable Zone:**
    - While the habitable zone is a useful concept for identifying potentially habitable environments, it should not be considered the sole criterion for life.
    - Planets outside the habitable zone, such as those in the outer regions or with different atmospheric compositions, may still harbor conditions conducive to life.

The concept of the habitable zone provides a starting point for assessing the potential habitability of exoplanets. However, as our understanding of planetary systems and the requirements for life evolves, it is important to consider a broader range of factors and explore the possibilities of habitability beyond the traditional boundaries of the habitable zone.

Stellar Class and Its Influence on Habitable Zones

The type and characteristics of a star, specifically its spectral class, play a significant role in determining the boundaries and conditions of the habitable zone around it. Here, we explore how stellar class influences the habitable zone:

1. **Spectral Classes and Luminosity:**
    - Stars are classified into different spectral classes based on their temperatures, which in turn affects their luminosity and energy output.
    - The main spectral classes, from hottest to coolest, are O, B, A, F, G, K, and M, with O being the hottest and M being the coolest.

2. **The Effect of Stellar Class on the Habitable Zone:**
    - Stars with higher temperatures, such as O, B, and A-type stars, have higher luminosities and emit more energy.
    - As a result, the habitable zone around these stars will be located farther away to maintain the right conditions for liquid water, as they have a higher energy output.

3. **Main Sequence Stars and Habitable Zones:**
    - Main sequence stars, such as G-type stars like our Sun, are often considered prime candidates for hosting habitable planets with potentially Earth-like conditions.

- G-type stars have a moderate temperature and luminosity, providing a stable energy output that can sustain liquid water within their habitable zones.

4. **The Influence of Red Dwarf Stars:**
    - Red dwarf stars, classified as M-type stars, are the most common type of star in the galaxy.
    - They have lower temperatures and luminosities compared to G-type stars like the Sun.
    - The habitable zones around red dwarfs are significantly closer to the star due to their lower energy output, and planets within this zone are subject to tidal locking and increased stellar activity.

5. **Variations and Uncertainties:**
    - While the spectral class of a star provides a general understanding of its influence on the habitable zone, there can be variations and uncertainties.
    - Factors such as a star's age, mass, and metallicity can affect its luminosity and energy output, leading to variations in the habitable zone's boundaries.
    - Additionally, interactions between stellar radiation, planetary atmospheres, and geological processes can further complicate the picture.

Understanding the influence of stellar class on habitable zones helps astronomers in their search for potentially habitable exoplanets. By considering the characteristics of different types of stars, such as their temperature, luminosity, and energy output, scientists can refine their search and focus on systems that have the potential to host planets within their habitable zones. However, it is essential to consider other factors, such as the planet's atmosphere and composition, to comprehensively assess a planet's habitability.

Planetary Factors: Size, Composition, and Orbit

While the type and characteristics of a star are important in defining the habitable zone, several planetary factors also influence the potential habitability of a planet within that zone. Here, we explore the role of planetary size, composition, and orbit:

1. **Planetary Size:**
    - The size of a planet, specifically its radius and mass, affects its overall structure, composition, and geological activity.
    - Larger planets, such as gas giants, may have a different internal structure and atmosphere that make them unsuitable for hosting life as we know it.

- Earth-sized or smaller planets, referred to as terrestrial planets, are often considered more conducive to supporting life due to their solid surfaces and potential for maintaining an atmosphere.

2. **Planetary Composition:**

    - The composition of a planet, including its elemental makeup and the presence of key compounds, can influence its habitability.
    - Elements such as carbon, hydrogen, oxygen, nitrogen, and sulfur are essential building blocks of life as we know it.
    - The presence of compounds like water, organic molecules, and minerals can provide the necessary ingredients and environments for life to thrive.

3. **Orbit and Distance from the Star:**

    - The distance of a planet from its star, as determined by its orbit, is crucial for its habitability.
    - Planets within the habitable zone are typically at an optimal distance from their star, allowing for the right amount of stellar radiation to maintain liquid water on their surfaces.
    - Planets too close may experience excessive heating, leading to the loss of water through evaporation, while those too far may experience freezing temperatures and the lack of liquid water.

4. **Orbital Stability:**

    - The stability of a planet's orbit is important for maintaining a relatively stable climate over long periods.
    - Perturbations caused by other planets or external factors can disrupt an orbit and lead to extreme variations in temperature or atmospheric conditions, making it challenging for life to thrive.

5. **Atmosphere and Climate Regulation:**

    - The presence of an atmosphere and its composition greatly influences a planet's climate and habitability.
    - An atmosphere helps regulate temperature, distribute heat, and protect against harmful radiation.
    - Factors such as greenhouse gases, cloud cover, and atmospheric circulation patterns can impact a planet's overall climate and habitability.

Understanding the interplay between these planetary factors is crucial when assessing the potential habitability of exoplanets. While the habitable zone provides a general framework, the specific characteristics of a planet, including its size, composition, and orbital properties, must be considered to determine its suitability for hosting life. By studying these factors, scientists can refine their search for potentially habitable worlds and focus on those that exhibit favorable conditions for the emergence and sustenance of life.

Promising Exoplanets

Proxima Centauri b and the Quest for Closest Habitable Exoplanet

Proxima Centauri b, often referred to as Proxima b, is an exoplanet located in the habitable zone of the closest star to our solar system, Proxima Centauri. Here, we delve into the significance of Proxima Centauri b and the ongoing quest to discover the closest potentially habitable exoplanet:

1. **Discovery and Basic Information:**
   - Proxima Centauri b was discovered in 2016 using the radial velocity method, which detects the gravitational pull of a planet on its host star.
   - It orbits Proxima Centauri, a red dwarf star, with an orbital period of approximately 11.2 Earth days.
   - It has a minimum mass around 1.17 times that of Earth, making it an Earth-sized or slightly larger planet.

2. **Habitable Zone and Potential for Liquid Water:**
   - Proxima Centauri b is located within the habitable zone of its host star, where the conditions may be suitable for liquid water to exist on its surface.
   - Its proximity to its star raises questions about its potential for tidal locking, where one side of the planet always faces the star, leading to extreme temperature variations.

3. **Challenges and Limitations:**
   - Proxima Centauri is an active red dwarf star that exhibits frequent flares and stellar activity, which can have significant impacts on the planet's atmosphere and habitability.
   - The planet's close proximity to its star makes it challenging to study its atmosphere and determine its composition.

4. **Follow-up Studies and Future Exploration:**
   - Scientists are actively engaged in follow-up studies to gather more information about Proxima Centauri b.
   - These studies involve the use of advanced telescopes and instruments, such as the James Webb Space Telescope, to characterize its atmosphere and search for potential biosignatures.

5. **Importance in the Search for Life:**

    - Proxima Centauri b holds immense significance in the quest for finding a potentially habitable exoplanet in our cosmic neighborhood.

    - Its proximity to Earth makes it a target for future interstellar exploration and potential robotic missions to study its atmosphere, climate, and potential for life.

While Proxima Centauri b represents an exciting prospect for the search for extraterrestrial life, further research and advancements in observational techniques are necessary to unlock the mysteries surrounding its habitability and potential for hosting life. Continued exploration of Proxima Centauri b and other promising exoplanets will shed light on the diversity and potential prevalence of habitable environments beyond our solar system.

TRAPPIST-1 System and Its Multiple Potentially Habitable Planets

The TRAPPIST-1 system has garnered significant attention in the search for potentially habitable exoplanets due to its remarkable configuration of multiple Earth-sized planets orbiting a single star. Here, we explore the TRAPPIST-1 system and its implications for the search for habitable worlds:

1. **Discovery and Basic Information:**

    - The TRAPPIST-1 system was discovered in 2016 using the transit method, which detects slight dips in the star's brightness as planets pass in front of it.

    - It is located approximately 39 light-years away in the constellation Aquarius.

    - The star, TRAPPIST-1, is an ultra-cool dwarf star, significantly smaller and cooler than our Sun.

2. **The Seven Earth-sized Planets:**

    - The TRAPPIST-1 system consists of seven known planets, labeled TRAPPIST-1b through TRAPPIST-1h, with orbital periods ranging from 1.5 to 19 days.

    - These planets are all roughly Earth-sized, with masses and radii similar to or slightly larger than Earth.

3. **Potential Habitability and Characteristics:**

    - Three of the planets, TRAPPIST-1e, f, and g, are located within the star's habitable zone, where conditions may be suitable for liquid water to exist on the surface.

    - The proximity of the planets to their host star raises questions about tidal locking and the potential for habitable conditions on the permanent day-night terminator zone.

4. **Follow-up Studies and Atmospheric Characterization:**

    - Intensive follow-up observations, including with the Hubble Space Telescope and the James Webb Space Telescope (JWST), aim to study the atmospheres of the TRAPPIST-1 planets.
    - Analyzing the composition of their atmospheres will provide insights into their potential habitability and the presence of key molecules such as water vapor, methane, and oxygen.

5. **Importance and Future Exploration:**

    - The TRAPPIST-1 system presents a unique opportunity to study terrestrial exoplanets that may have conditions suitable for life.
    - The system serves as a testing ground for theories about planetary formation and evolution, as well as the potential prevalence of habitable environments in the galaxy.
    - Future missions, such as the JWST and advanced ground-based telescopes, will provide more detailed observations, enabling a deeper understanding of these intriguing worlds.

The TRAPPIST-1 system stands as a fascinating example of a planetary system with multiple potentially habitable planets. Further studies of the TRAPPIST-1 planets' atmospheres and surface conditions will contribute to our understanding of the factors necessary for habitability and the potential diversity of life-sustaining environments in the universe.

Kepler-452b: Earth's "Cousin" and Its Similarities to Our Planet

Kepler-452b is an exoplanet that has garnered attention for its similarities to Earth, earning it the nickname "Earth's Cousin." In this entry, we explore the characteristics of Kepler-452b and its intriguing similarities to our home planet:

1. **Discovery and Basic Information:**

    - Kepler-452b was discovered by NASA's Kepler spacecraft in 2015 using the transit method, which detects the periodic dimming of a star as a planet passes in front of it.
    - It is located approximately 1,400 light-years away in the constellation Cygnus.
    - Kepler-452b orbits a star similar to our Sun, known as Kepler-452, with an orbital period of approximately 385 days.

2. **Earth-Like Characteristics:**

    - Kepler-452b is classified as a "super-Earth," as it is about 1.5 times the size of Earth and has a mass estimated to be around five times that of Earth.

- It resides within the habitable zone of its star, where conditions may be suitable for liquid water to exist on its surface.

3. **Orbital and Stellar Similarities:**
    - Kepler-452b's orbital period is remarkably similar to Earth's, suggesting a comparable yearly cycle.
    - Its host star, Kepler-452, is slightly larger and older than our Sun, with a similar temperature and spectral type.

4. **Potential Habitability:**
    - The presence of an exoplanet with Earth-like characteristics raises the possibility of a habitable environment.
    - Kepler-452b's location within the habitable zone indicates that it receives a similar amount of stellar radiation as Earth, potentially allowing for stable surface temperatures.

5. **Challenges and Limitations:**
    - Despite its similarities to Earth, there are still many unknowns about Kepler-452b.
    - Detailed studies of its atmosphere and surface conditions are challenging due to the significant distance and current limitations in observational capabilities.

6. **Significance and Future Exploration:**
    - Kepler-452b offers valuable insights into the potential prevalence of Earth-like planets in the universe.
    - Further advancements in technology and future space missions may enable us to probe the atmosphere of Kepler-452b, searching for signs of life and gaining a deeper understanding of its habitability.

Kepler-452b stands as an intriguing exoplanet with similarities to our own planet, offering valuable clues in the search for habitable worlds beyond our solar system. While further research and observations are needed to unravel its mysteries, Kepler-452b serves as a reminder of the vast possibilities in our cosmic neighborhood and the potential for finding Earth-like environments among the stars.

Life Beyond Carbon

Alternative Biochemistries
Silicon-Based Life and Its Theoretical Viability

In the quest to understand the potential diversity of life in the universe, scientists have explored the concept of alternative biochemistries. One such intriguing possibility is silicon-based life. In this entry, we delve into the theoretical viability of silicon-based life forms:

1. **Carbon and Silicon as Building Blocks of Life:**

    - Carbon, with its unique bonding properties, is the foundation of organic chemistry and the basis for life on Earth.

    - Silicon, located below carbon in the periodic table, shares some chemical similarities with carbon and has the potential to form stable bonds.

2. **Silicon's Potential for Life:**

    - Silicon-based life refers to the hypothetical existence of organisms whose biochemistry relies on silicon compounds instead of carbon compounds.

    - Silicon has a larger atomic radius than carbon, which allows for more complex structures and potential stability in certain environments.

3. **Challenges and Limitations:**

    - While silicon shares some chemical properties with carbon, it also possesses distinct differences that present significant challenges for life.

    - Silicon-based compounds tend to be less versatile and reactive compared to carbon-based compounds.

    - Silicon also has a lower propensity to form stable, complex molecules essential for biological processes.

4. **Extreme Environments and Silicon-Based Life:**

    - The potential viability of silicon-based life forms has been explored in extreme environments, such as high temperatures, pressures, or acidic conditions.

    - In these environments, silicon-based compounds may exhibit greater stability and reactivity compared to standard terrestrial conditions.

5. **Experimental and Theoretical Studies:**

    - Scientists have conducted laboratory experiments and theoretical studies to investigate the behavior and potential of silicon-based compounds.

    - These studies aim to understand the stability, reactivity, and possible biochemistry of silicon-based life forms.

6. **Speculation and Future Research:**
    - While silicon-based life remains theoretical, it sparks intriguing speculation about the possibilities of biochemistries beyond carbon-based life.
    - Continued research, experimentation, and advancements in understanding the properties of silicon-based compounds will provide valuable insights into the potential for alternative forms of life.

While the viability of silicon-based life forms remains uncertain, the exploration of alternative biochemistries expands our understanding of the fundamental requirements for life and the potential diversity of life forms in the universe. Silicon-based life serves as a thought-provoking concept that challenges our assumptions and opens up new avenues for scientific exploration.

Arsenic-Based Life and Controversial Findings

In the search for alternative biochemistries, arsenic-based life has been a topic of scientific investigation. Arsenic, an element located near phosphorus on the periodic table, has properties that make it a potential candidate for supporting life. However, the findings regarding arsenic-based life have been controversial. Here, we explore the research and controversies surrounding this intriguing concept:

1. **Arsenic and Its Chemical Properties:**
    - Arsenic is a semi-metallic element with chemical properties that partially resemble phosphorus, a key element in biological molecules like DNA and RNA.
    - Arsenic has the ability to form stable bonds and interact with other elements in ways similar to phosphorus.

2. **The NASA Study:**
    - In 2010, a NASA-funded study led by Felisa Wolfe-Simon reported the discovery of a bacterium called GFAJ-1 that appeared to incorporate arsenic into its DNA instead of phosphorus.
    - The study suggested that GFAJ-1 could survive and replicate under high arsenic concentrations, challenging the assumption that life is exclusively based on carbon, hydrogen, nitrogen, oxygen, phosphorus, and sulfur (CHNOPS).

3. **Scientific Criticism and Controversies:**
    - The NASA study received widespread attention and sparked significant debate within the scientific community.
    - Many scientists raised concerns about the methodology and interpretation of the study's results, questioning whether arsenic truly replaced phosphorus in the DNA of GFAJ-1.

- Several subsequent studies failed to replicate the findings, casting doubt on the initial claims.

4. **Lessons Learned and Continuing Research:**

    - The controversy surrounding arsenic-based life highlights the importance of rigorous scientific scrutiny and reproducibility in experimental studies.

    - The failed attempts to reproduce the results have led researchers to conclude that the initial findings were likely due to contamination or other factors, rather than genuine evidence of arsenic-based life.

5. **Future Directions:**

    - Despite the controversy, the concept of alternative biochemistries remains an intriguing area of research.

    - Scientists continue to explore the possibilities of elements other than carbon, hydrogen, nitrogen, oxygen, phosphorus, and sulfur in the building blocks of life.

    - Advances in experimental techniques and astrobiology research may shed further light on the potential for alternative biochemistries.

While the initial claims of arsenic-based life generated significant excitement, subsequent investigations and critical evaluations have cast doubt on the validity of those findings. The controversies surrounding arsenic-based life serve as a reminder of the importance of rigorous scientific inquiry and the need for multiple lines of evidence before accepting extraordinary claims. The quest to understand alternative biochemistries and the potential for diverse forms of life in the universe continues to stimulate scientific curiosity and exploration.

Non-Replicating Genetic Polymers as Potential Building Blocks

In the exploration of alternative biochemistries, non-replicating genetic polymers have emerged as intriguing candidates for serving as building blocks of life. These polymers, distinct from the nucleic acids found in Earth-based life, offer insights into the possibilities of alternative genetic systems. Here, we delve into the concept of non-replicating genetic polymers and their potential as fundamental components of life:

1. **Non-Replicating Genetic Polymers:**

    - Non-replicating genetic polymers refer to molecular structures that possess genetic information but do not undergo the replication process observed in DNA and RNA.

    - These polymers may have distinct chemical compositions and functionalities compared to the nucleic acids commonly found in terrestrial life.

2. **Diversity of Non-Replicating Genetic Polymers:**
   - Various types of non-replicating genetic polymers have been proposed and studied, including peptide nucleic acids (PNAs), threose nucleic acids (TNAs), and glycol nucleic acids (GNAs).
   - These polymers can exhibit unique properties such as stability, versatility, and the ability to store and transfer genetic information.

3. **Synthetic Approaches and Laboratory Studies:**
   - Scientists have synthesized non-replicating genetic polymers in the laboratory using organic chemistry techniques.
   - These studies aim to understand the properties, stability, and potential functionalities of these polymers as genetic carriers.

4. **Potential Advantages and Challenges:**
   - Non-replicating genetic polymers offer potential advantages in terms of stability under extreme conditions and diverse chemical functionalities.
   - However, their complex synthesis and limited understanding of their interactions with other biological molecules present challenges in assessing their viability as fundamental components of life.

5. **Origins of Non-Replicating Genetic Polymers:**
   - Exploring the origins of non-replicating genetic polymers is essential in understanding their potential role in the emergence of life.
   - Studying the environments of early Earth, meteorites, and other celestial bodies may provide insights into the conditions that could support the formation of these polymers.

6. **Implications for Astrobiology:**
   - Investigating non-replicating genetic polymers expands our understanding of the diversity of possible genetic systems beyond DNA and RNA.
   - It offers insights into the potential for alternative biochemistries and the range of building blocks that could support life in different environments.

While non-replicating genetic polymers present intriguing possibilities for alternative genetic systems, further research is needed to fully understand their properties, functions, and potential contributions to the emergence and sustainability of life. The exploration of non-replicating genetic polymers broadens our perspectives on the nature of life and underscores the vast array of possibilities that may exist beyond the familiar genetic systems found on Earth.

Extreme Environments on Earth
Extremophiles in Acidic Environments

Extreme environments on Earth harbor a remarkable diversity of life, challenging our traditional understanding of habitable conditions. Acidic environments, characterized by low pH levels, are home to a unique group of extremophiles. In this entry, we explore the fascinating world of extremophiles thriving in acidic environments:

1. **Acidic Environments:**

    - Acidic environments are characterized by low pH levels (below 7) due to the presence of acidic compounds, such as sulfuric acid or hydrochloric acid.

    - These environments include natural settings like acid mine drainage sites, volcanic hot springs, and acidified lakes.

2. **Acidophilic Extremophiles:**

    - Acidophilic extremophiles are organisms that thrive in highly acidic conditions, sometimes approaching or even surpassing pH 0.

    - They have evolved unique adaptations to survive and function in these challenging environments.

3. **Types of Acidophilic Extremophiles:**

    - Acidophilic bacteria: Certain bacteria, such as Acidithiobacillus and Acidiphilium, are well-adapted to acidic environments and play essential roles in biogeochemical cycles.

    - Acidophilic archaea: Acidophilic archaea, such as Ferroplasma and Sulfolobus, are capable of thriving in highly acidic conditions, utilizing various energy sources and displaying diverse metabolic capabilities.

4. **Adaptations to Acidic Environments:**

    - Acid-stable enzymes: Acidophilic extremophiles produce enzymes that remain functional and stable at low pH levels, enabling them to carry out vital biological processes.

    - Acid-resistant cell membranes: These organisms possess specialized cell membranes that can withstand the corrosive effects of acid.

    - Efficient pH regulation: Acidophiles have efficient mechanisms for maintaining internal pH homeostasis, preventing cellular damage caused by extreme acidity.

5. **Ecological Significance:**
    - Acidophilic extremophiles play crucial roles in natural acidified environments, contributing to biogeochemical cycles and ecosystem dynamics.
    - They participate in processes such as sulfur and iron oxidation, helping to shape the chemistry and mineralogy of acidic habitats.

6. **Astrobiological Implications:**
    - Studying extremophiles in acidic environments on Earth provides insights into the potential habitability of acidic environments on other planets or moons, such as Mars or Jupiter's moon Io.
    - Understanding the adaptations of acidophilic extremophiles can inform our search for life in extreme environments beyond Earth.

The study of extremophiles in acidic environments expands our understanding of the remarkable adaptability and resilience of life on Earth. Acidophilic extremophiles serve as intriguing models for exploring the limits of life and the potential for habitability in extreme environments, both on our planet and beyond.

Life in High-Temperature Environments

Life on Earth has demonstrated its incredible adaptability by thriving in extreme high-temperature environments. These habitats, characterized by intense heat and thermal fluctuations, are home to a diverse range of organisms known as thermophiles. In this entry, we explore the fascinating adaptations and significance of life in high-temperature environments:

1. **High-Temperature Environments:**
    - High-temperature environments, also known as thermophilic habitats, are characterized by extreme heat, often exceeding the typical temperature range for most organisms.
    - Examples of high-temperature environments include hydrothermal vents, hot springs, geothermal areas, and volcanic regions.

2. **Thermophiles:**
    - Thermophiles are organisms that thrive and reproduce optimally in high-temperature conditions, typically above 45°C (113°F) and even surpassing 80°C (176°F) in some cases.
    - They belong to various domains of life, including bacteria, archaea, and even some eukaryotes.

3. **Adaptations to High-Temperature Environments:**

    - Thermostable enzymes: Thermophiles produce enzymes that remain stable and functional at high temperatures. These enzymes have applications in various industries, including biotechnology and molecular biology.

    - Heat-resistant cell membranes: Organisms in high-temperature environments possess unique cell membrane compositions and structures that can withstand thermal stress.

    - DNA stabilization: Thermophiles have mechanisms to stabilize their DNA, preventing thermal denaturation and maintaining genetic integrity.

    - Efficient energy metabolism: These organisms have evolved energy metabolism systems that can function optimally at high temperatures.

4. **Examples of High-Temperature Environments:**

    - Hydrothermal vents: These deep-sea environments, characterized by volcanic activity and extreme pressure, host thermophilic communities fueled by chemosynthesis.

    - Hot springs: Geothermal areas with hot springs, such as the geysers of Yellowstone National Park, provide habitats for diverse thermophilic microorganisms.

    - Volcanic regions: Some volcanic areas, such as the slopes of active volcanoes, harbor thermophiles adapted to the high temperatures and mineral-rich conditions.

5. **Ecological Significance:**

    - Thermophiles play important roles in the biogeochemical cycles of high-temperature environments, including the cycling of sulfur, iron, and other elements.

    - They contribute to the production of minerals and participate in the degradation of organic matter, influencing ecosystem dynamics in these extreme habitats.

6. **Astrobiological Implications:**

    - Studying thermophiles expands our understanding of the limits of life and the potential for habitability in high-temperature environments on other planets or moons, such as the subsurface oceans of icy moons like Enceladus or Europa.

    - Thermophilic organisms offer insights into the survival strategies and biochemical adaptations that might be necessary for life in extreme conditions elsewhere in the universe.

Life in high-temperature environments challenges our preconceived notions of habitable conditions and underscores the adaptability of life on Earth. Thermophiles serve as fascinating models for understanding the limits of life and exploring the potential for habitability in extreme environments, both on our planet and in the search for life beyond Earth.

Organisms Thriving in High-Pressure Conditions

While most life on Earth is adapted to ambient pressure conditions, certain organisms have evolved to thrive in high-pressure environments, such as the deep sea and hydrothermal vents. In this entry, we explore the fascinating adaptations and significance of organisms that can withstand and even thrive under extreme pressure:

1. **High-Pressure Environments:**

    - High-pressure environments refer to regions where organisms are subjected to pressures exceeding atmospheric pressure.

    - These environments include the deep sea, trenches, subterranean habitats, and areas near hydrothermal vents.

2. **Piezophiles and Barophiles:**

    - Piezophiles, also known as barophiles, are organisms that are specifically adapted to high-pressure conditions.

    - They have evolved unique mechanisms to withstand and function optimally under the intense pressure in their habitats.

3. **Adaptations to High-Pressure Environments:**

    - Membrane adaptations: Organisms in high-pressure environments have specialized cell membranes that maintain integrity and prevent leakage of cellular components.

    - Enzyme stability: Piezophiles produce enzymes that remain stable and functional under high-pressure conditions, allowing for efficient biochemical reactions.

    - Pressure-regulating mechanisms: These organisms have developed mechanisms to regulate internal pressure, maintaining cellular homeostasis in high-pressure environments.

    - Molecular adaptations: Specific adaptations at the molecular level, such as modifications to proteins and nucleic acids, help maintain their structural integrity and function.

4. **Deep-Sea Organisms:**

    - Deep-sea environments, characterized by high hydrostatic pressure, low temperatures, and limited light, harbor diverse organisms adapted to these conditions.

- Examples include deep-sea bacteria, archaea, and invertebrates like deep-sea fish, squid, and shrimp.

5. **Hydrothermal Vent Organisms:**

    - Hydrothermal vents, found in the deep sea near volcanic activity, support unique ecosystems with organisms adapted to high pressure, high temperatures, and chemically rich environments.

    - These ecosystems include tube worms, vent crabs, and other species that rely on chemosynthetic bacteria for their energy needs.

6. **Significance and Astrobiological Implications:**

    - Understanding the adaptations of organisms thriving in high-pressure environments on Earth can inform our search for life in similar conditions on other planets, such as icy moons like Europa or Enceladus.

    - The study of piezophiles offers insights into the limits of life and the potential for habitability in extreme pressure environments beyond Earth.

Organisms thriving in high-pressure conditions demonstrate the remarkable adaptability of life on Earth. The exploration of these environments and the organisms that inhabit them provide valuable insights into the limits of life and the potential for habitability in extreme pressure environments, expanding our understanding of the diverse forms life may take in the universe.

Implications for Extraterrestrial Life

Extremophiles as Analogues for Extraterrestrial Life

Extremophiles, organisms that thrive in extreme environments on Earth, have captured the attention of scientists studying the potential for extraterrestrial life. In this entry, we explore how extremophiles serve as valuable analogues for understanding the possibilities and conditions for life beyond Earth:

1. **Extremophiles and Their Diversity:**

    - Extremophiles are organisms that have evolved to live in extreme conditions that were once thought to be inhospitable for life.

    - They can be found in various extreme environments, including high temperatures, acidic or alkaline conditions, high-pressure environments, and even locations with high levels of radiation.

2. **Adaptations to Extreme Environments:**

    - Extremophiles possess unique adaptations that allow them to survive and thrive in their extreme habitats.

- These adaptations include specialized enzymes and proteins, membrane structures, DNA repair mechanisms, and metabolic processes that enable them to tolerate or even utilize extreme conditions.

3. **Analogies to Extraterrestrial Environments:**

    - Extremophiles provide valuable analogies for the conditions that may exist on other planets, moons, or celestial bodies in our solar system and beyond.
    - By studying extremophiles, scientists can gain insights into the limits and possibilities of life in environments that were once considered inhospitable.

4. **Astrobiological Significance:**

    - Extremophiles inform the search for extraterrestrial life by expanding our understanding of the range of habitable conditions.
    - They provide clues about the potential for life in extreme environments on other planets or moons, such as Mars, Europa, Enceladus, or the icy moons of Jupiter and Saturn.
    - Extremophiles serve as models for studying the potential biochemical adaptations and survival strategies that may be necessary for life in unique environments.

5. **Technological Applications:**

    - Extremophiles have practical applications in fields such as biotechnology, medicine, and astrobiology.
    - Their unique enzymes and proteins can be used in various industrial processes, including the production of biofuels, bioremediation of contaminated sites, and the development of extremozymes for extreme conditions.

6. **Future Directions:**

    - Continued exploration and study of extremophiles on Earth will enhance our understanding of the conditions that support life.
    - Future missions and research endeavors will focus on identifying and characterizing extremophiles in extreme environments on Earth and extending the search for life to other planetary bodies.

Extremophiles offer valuable insights into the possibilities and conditions for life beyond Earth. By studying these remarkable organisms, scientists can refine their understanding of habitability and enhance the search for life in extreme environments, both within our solar system and in the broader context of the universe.

Constraints and Adaptations of Alternative Biochemistries

While carbon-based life forms dominate Earth, the exploration of alternative biochemistries broadens our understanding of the potential diversity of life in the universe. However, alternative biochemistries face unique constraints and require specific adaptations to sustain life. In this entry, we delve into the constraints and adaptations associated with alternative biochemistries:

1. **Non-Carbon-Based Biochemistries:**

    - Alternative biochemistries propose the use of elements other than carbon as the backbone for molecular structures.

    - Silicon, boron, arsenic, and even non-replicating genetic polymers have been suggested as potential alternatives to carbon-based life.

2. **Constraints and Challenges:**

    - Availability of elements: The abundance of elements in a planetary system affects the likelihood of their incorporation into alternative biochemistries.

    - Chemical stability: Elements used in alternative biochemistries must form stable and functional compounds that can withstand the environmental conditions of the habitat.

    - Energy requirements: Alternative biochemistries must find suitable energy sources to sustain life processes and enable metabolic reactions.

3. **Adaptations to Alternative Biochemistries:**

    - Molecular structures: Organisms in alternative biochemistries must develop molecular structures that are stable and functional under their specific elemental compositions.

    - Metabolism and energy utilization: Alternative biochemistries require unique metabolic pathways and energy utilization mechanisms that are compatible with the specific elements involved.

    - Replication and inheritance: Alternative biochemistries may involve alternative genetic systems or mechanisms for replication and inheritance of genetic information.

4. **Environmental Constraints:**

    - Habitability considerations: The conditions necessary to support alternative biochemistries differ from those required for carbon-based life.

    - Temperature and pressure ranges, solvent properties, and the presence of suitable elements and compounds play crucial roles in determining the habitability of environments for alternative biochemistries.

5. **Astrobiological Significance:**

    - Studying alternative biochemistries expands our understanding of the possibilities for life in the universe, including the potential habitability of exoplanets and moons.

    - It informs the development of biosignatures and detection methods that can be used to search for signs of alternative biochemistries beyond Earth.

6. **Experimental and Theoretical Investigations:**

    - Laboratory experiments and theoretical models are used to explore the viability and limitations of alternative biochemistries.

    - By simulating different environmental conditions and examining the chemical properties of alternative elements, scientists aim to understand the constraints and adaptations required for alternative biochemistries.

The study of alternative biochemistries provides insights into the potential diversity of life in the universe and challenges our preconceived notions about the requirements for habitability. While much remains to be explored and understood, investigating the constraints and adaptations of alternative biochemistries opens new avenues in astrobiology and enhances our quest for extraterrestrial life.

Prospects of Discovering Non-Carbon-Based Life in the Universe

The search for life beyond Earth traditionally focuses on carbon-based life forms due to their prevalence on our planet. However, the exploration of non-carbon-based life opens up exciting possibilities for discovering alternative forms of life in the universe. In this entry, we explore the prospects of discovering non-carbon-based life and the implications it would have for our understanding of biology and astrobiology:

1. **Expanding the Definition of Life:**

    - Discovering non-carbon-based life would challenge our current definition of life, which is largely based on the biochemistry of carbon-based organisms.

    - It would necessitate a reevaluation and expansion of the fundamental criteria used to define and identify life.

2. **Alternative Biochemistries:**

    - Non-carbon-based life may utilize elements such as silicon, boron, or even exotic elements not commonly associated with life on Earth.

    - These alternative biochemistries would involve different molecular structures, metabolic processes, and genetic systems compared to carbon-based life.

3. **Habitability Considerations:**
   - Identifying potential environments that could support non-carbon-based life is crucial.
   - The availability of suitable elements, energy sources, and stable environmental conditions would play a significant role in determining the habitability of specific locations.

4. **Biosignatures and Detection Methods:**
   - Discovering non-carbon-based life would require the development of new biosignatures and detection methods.
   - Traditional approaches that rely on carbon-based biomarkers may not be applicable, necessitating innovative strategies to identify the unique signatures of alternative biochemistries.

5. **Extreme Environments:**
   - Non-carbon-based life may be more likely to thrive in extreme environments where conditions are drastically different from Earth.
   - Such environments include high temperatures, extreme pressures, or chemically hostile conditions that would be inhospitable to carbon-based life.

6. **Technological Advancements:**
   - Advancements in technology, including remote sensing, spectroscopy, and sample return missions, would greatly enhance our ability to detect and study non-carbon-based life forms.
   - These technological developments would enable us to explore a wider range of environments and increase the chances of discovering alternative biochemistries.

7. **Implications for Astrobiology:**
   - The discovery of non-carbon-based life would revolutionize our understanding of biology and the possibilities for life in the universe.
   - It would challenge our assumptions about the requirements for life and open up new avenues of research in astrobiology.

While the search for non-carbon-based life remains speculative, the prospects of discovering such lifeforms expand our horizons and push the boundaries of our knowledge. Exploring alternative biochemistries enhances our understanding of the diversity of life and the potential for habitability in the universe, ultimately leading to profound insights into the nature of life itself.

Communication with Extraterrestrial Life

The Search for Intelligent Extraterrestrial Civilizations (SETI)

History of SETI Initiatives

The history of SETI initiatives traces humanity's ongoing quest to detect signs of intelligent extraterrestrial civilizations. Over the years, numerous projects and milestones have contributed to the development of the Search for Intelligent Extraterrestrial Civilizations (SETI). This entry provides an overview of the key moments and initiatives in the history of SETI:

1. **Early Speculations:**

    - The idea of searching for intelligent life beyond Earth dates back centuries.
    - Early philosophers and thinkers, such as Giordano Bruno and Johannes Kepler, proposed the existence of other inhabited worlds.

2. **Project Ozma:**

    - Project Ozma, led by astronomer Frank Drake in 1960, is considered the first modern SETI initiative.
    - Using a radio telescope, Drake conducted the first systematic search for extraterrestrial radio signals from the star system Tau Ceti.

3. **The Drake Equation:**

    - The Drake Equation, formulated by Frank Drake in 1961, quantifies the factors affecting the number of communicative civilizations in our galaxy.
    - It considers variables such as the rate of star formation, the fraction of stars with planets, and the likelihood of life emerging on habitable planets.

4. **The Search for Extraterrestrial Intelligence (SETI):**

    - In 1974, a notable SETI project called the Arecibo message was transmitted from the Arecibo Observatory in Puerto Rico.
    - The Arecibo message was a binary-coded pictorial representation of humanity and Earth's location sent towards the globular star cluster M13.

5. **Project Phoenix:**

    - Project Phoenix, initiated in 1995, was a major SETI effort that employed sophisticated radio telescopes to survey nearby sun-like stars.
    - Its goal was to search for narrowband signals indicative of extraterrestrial technology.

6. **The SETI@home Project:**

    - SETI@home, launched in 1999, utilized distributed computing to harness the power of volunteers' personal computers for data analysis.

- Participants could contribute their idle computer processing power to analyze radio telescope data for potential signals.

7. **The Breakthrough Initiatives:**

    - The Breakthrough Initiatives, announced in 2015 by entrepreneur Yuri Milner, are a series of ambitious projects aimed at advancing the search for extraterrestrial intelligence.
    - Breakthrough Listen, one of the initiatives, conducts comprehensive and targeted SETI surveys using some of the world's most powerful telescopes.

Throughout the history of SETI, these initiatives and others have propelled our understanding of the search for intelligent extraterrestrial civilizations. They have shaped the methods, technologies, and strategies employed in the ongoing quest for conclusive evidence of communication from civilizations beyond Earth. The next entries in this chapter will delve into the specific techniques and approaches used in SETI, highlighting the ongoing efforts to detect signals from intelligent beings in the cosmos.

Radio Signal Detection and Analysis

One of the primary methods used in the search for intelligent extraterrestrial civilizations (SETI) is the detection and analysis of radio signals. Radio waves are an attractive means of communication across vast distances due to their ability to travel through space with minimal degradation. This entry explores the techniques and processes involved in radio signal detection and analysis in the context of SETI:

1. **Radio Telescope Arrays:**

    - Radio telescopes are instrumental in the search for extraterrestrial radio signals.
    - SETI projects often utilize arrays of radio telescopes to increase sensitivity and improve signal detection capabilities.
    - Examples of such arrays include the Allen Telescope Array (ATA) and the Very Large Array (VLA).

2. **Target Selection:**

    - SETI initiatives focus on specific target stars or regions of the sky that are considered promising for the presence of intelligent life.
    - Criteria for target selection may include factors such as proximity, star type, and the presence of exoplanets within the star's habitable zone.

3. **Signal Detection:**

    - Radio signals from space can be detected using radio telescopes tuned to specific frequencies.

- SETI searches typically involve scanning a broad range of frequencies in the radio spectrum, including the so-called "water hole" frequencies.
- Detection algorithms and signal processing techniques are employed to identify potential signals of interest.

4. **Narrowband and Wideband Signals:**

    - SETI searches often target narrowband signals, which are characterized by a concentrated energy within a narrow frequency range.
    - Narrowband signals are typically indicative of artificial origin since natural astrophysical sources tend to produce wideband signals.
    - Wideband signals, on the other hand, span a broader range of frequencies and can include both natural and artificial sources.

5. **Signal Analysis:**

    - Once a signal of interest is detected, thorough analysis is conducted to determine its potential significance.
    - Various parameters are assessed, including signal strength, duration, modulation, and frequency stability.
    - Signal verification and confirmation are crucial steps to distinguish potential candidate signals from noise or human-made interference.

6. **SETI Signal Classification:**

    - SETI signal classification involves categorizing detected signals based on their characteristics and likelihood of being of extraterrestrial origin.
    - Signals are classified into different types, such as single-pulse signals, continuous waveforms, or repetitive patterns, each requiring further investigation.

7. **Data Sharing and Collaboration:**

    - SETI projects often involve collaboration and data sharing among research institutions and organizations worldwide.
    - Sharing data enables cross-validation of findings and maximizes the chances of detecting and confirming potential extraterrestrial signals.

Radio signal detection and analysis continue to be key components of SETI efforts, combining advanced technologies, signal processing algorithms, and the collective efforts of researchers and citizen scientists. These ongoing endeavors bring us closer to the possibility of detecting signals from intelligent extraterrestrial civilizations and unraveling the mysteries of the universe.

Messaging and Active SETI Controversies

In the search for intelligent extraterrestrial civilizations (SETI), the concept of messaging and active SETI has sparked significant debates and controversies within the scientific community. This entry explores the different perspectives and considerations surrounding messaging attempts and active SETI initiatives:

1. **Messaging to Extraterrestrial Intelligence (METI):**

    - Messaging to Extraterrestrial Intelligence, or METI, refers to deliberate attempts by humans to send intentional signals to potential extraterrestrial civilizations.

    - METI initiatives aim to establish communication and initiate dialogue with hypothetical extraterrestrial beings.

    - Controversies surrounding METI revolve around concerns regarding the potential risks and ethical implications of broadcasting our presence to unknown civilizations.

2. **The "Silent" Approach:**

    - Some scientists argue in favor of the "silent" approach, where passive listening is prioritized over active broadcasting.

    - Proponents of the silent approach advocate caution, emphasizing the need to assess potential risks and consequences before intentionally transmitting signals into space.

    - The fear is that active broadcasting could attract the attention of potentially hostile or technologically superior civilizations.

3. **The Fermi Paradox and the "Zoo Hypothesis":**

    - The Fermi Paradox raises the question of why we have not yet detected any clear signs of extraterrestrial civilizations, given the vast number of potentially habitable worlds in the universe.

    - One proposed solution is the "Zoo Hypothesis," which suggests that extraterrestrial civilizations are intentionally avoiding contact with Earth and monitoring us from afar.

    - Active SETI initiatives could disrupt this hypothetical "zoo" scenario, potentially leading to unintended consequences.

4. **International Protocols and Concerns:**

    - Discussions within the scientific community have highlighted the need for international protocols and guidelines regarding active SETI activities.

- Concerns include the potential violation of ethical boundaries, the risk of cultural misunderstandings, and the impact of messages on less developed civilizations.
- The International Academy of Astronautics (IAA) has been involved in establishing principles and recommendations for conducting active SETI activities responsibly.

5. **Communication Standards and Message Content:**
    - In the event of intentional messaging, considerations regarding the content and format of the messages arise.
    - Discussions revolve around constructing messages that are understandable by potential extraterrestrial recipients and convey universal concepts.
    - Efforts are made to ensure that messages are encoded with basic scientific and mathematical principles to facilitate potential decipherment.

The controversies surrounding messaging and active SETI reflect the complex considerations and uncertainties involved in attempting interstellar communication. The debates focus on the potential risks, the need for international collaboration and consensus, and the ethical responsibility of humanity when engaging in such initiatives. As the search for intelligent extraterrestrial civilizations progresses, ongoing discussions and evaluations will shape the future of messaging efforts in the quest for contact with other worlds.

Challenges of Interstellar Communication

Limitations of Light-Speed and Interstellar Distances

Interstellar communication presents numerous challenges due to the vast distances involved and the limitations imposed by the speed of light. This entry explores the key limitations and considerations related to interstellar communication:

1. **Light-Speed Limit:**
    - The speed of light in a vacuum, approximately 299,792 kilometers per second (186,282 miles per second), sets a fundamental limit on the rate at which information can travel through space.
    - Interstellar distances are immense, and even at the speed of light, it takes years or centuries for signals to traverse these distances.

2. **Communication Delays:**
    - Due to the finite speed of light, interstellar communication suffers from significant delays.
    - For example, a message sent to a star located 10 light-years away would take 10 years to reach its destination, and the response would take an additional 10 years to return to the sender.

- Communication delays make real-time conversations across vast distances impractical or impossible.

3. **Signal Degradation:**
   - As electromagnetic signals propagate through space, they experience signal degradation and attenuation.
   - Factors such as interstellar dust, cosmic radiation, and background noise can weaken or distort the transmitted signals, making them difficult to interpret accurately.

4. **Power Requirements:**
   - Transmitting signals across interstellar distances requires significant amounts of power.
   - As signals propagate, their energy dissipates, necessitating powerful transmitters to maintain signal strength over vast distances.
   - Energy requirements for long-distance interstellar communication pose substantial technological challenges.

5. **Directed vs. Omnidirectional Communication:**
   - Interstellar communication requires careful consideration of the communication approach.
   - Omnidirectional signals, which radiate equally in all directions, become progressively weaker as they travel, limiting their effective range.
   - Directed communication, focused on specific target systems, can enhance signal strength and increase the chances of successful reception.

6. **Relativity and Time Dilation:**
   - The theory of relativity introduces additional complexities to interstellar communication.
   - Time dilation effects, caused by relative motion or gravitational fields, can lead to differences in the perceived passage of time between sender and receiver.
   - Coordinating communication over vast distances while accounting for time dilation effects adds another layer of complexity.

7. **Information Encoding and Decoding:**
   - Designing effective information encoding and decoding methods is crucial for interstellar communication.

- Ensuring that transmitted signals can be understood and deciphered by potential extraterrestrial recipients requires the use of universal principles and shared knowledge.

Interstellar communication faces formidable challenges due to the limitations imposed by the speed of light and the vastness of interstellar distances. Overcoming these challenges will require advancements in technology, innovative communication strategies, and a deeper understanding of fundamental physics. While interstellar communication remains a significant scientific and technological hurdle, ongoing research and future discoveries may one day enable meaningful exchanges with civilizations in distant star systems.

Communication Methods: Binary, Mathematical, Universal Constants

When attempting to establish interstellar communication, scientists have explored various communication methods that rely on universal concepts and principles. This entry discusses three commonly considered methods:

1. **Binary Communication:**
   - Binary communication involves using a binary code system to transmit information.
   - Binary code uses a combination of two symbols, typically represented as 0 and 1, to convey information.
   - This method relies on the assumption that an extraterrestrial intelligence would understand the concept of binary representation and be able to decipher the encoded message.

2. **Mathematical Communication:**
   - Mathematics is considered a universal language that transcends cultural and linguistic barriers.
   - Mathematical communication involves transmitting information using mathematical principles and concepts.
   - Concepts such as arithmetic, geometry, and algebra could be used to convey fundamental knowledge and establish a common understanding.

3. **Universal Constants and Physical Laws:**
   - Universal constants and fundamental physical laws are constants and principles that are believed to be the same throughout the universe.
   - Examples of universal constants include the speed of light, the gravitational constant, and the Planck constant.
   - By referencing these constants and laws, messages can convey shared knowledge and establish a basis for communication.

Each of these communication methods has its own strengths and limitations. Binary communication provides a straightforward and concise way of encoding information, but it relies on the assumption that extraterrestrial intelligences understand the binary system. Mathematical communication offers a universal language that is not reliant on specific symbols, but it requires shared mathematical knowledge. Referencing universal constants and physical laws can provide a common framework, but it may require a deep understanding of physics and mathematics on the part of both sender and receiver.

Successful interstellar communication will likely involve a combination of these methods, utilizing multiple approaches to convey a broader range of information. Additionally, efforts to establish communication protocols and shared conventions will be crucial to ensuring effective understanding and interpretation of messages.

As scientists continue to explore interstellar communication, advancements in technology and a deeper understanding of universal concepts will contribute to the development of more sophisticated and effective communication methods.

Technological Advancements and Future Possibilities

Technological advancements play a crucial role in the quest for communication with extraterrestrial life. As our understanding of science and engineering grows, new possibilities emerge. This entry explores some of the technological advancements and future possibilities in the field of interstellar communication:

1. **Advanced Radio Telescope Arrays:**

    - Radio telescopes are essential tools in the search for extraterrestrial signals.

    - Advancements in radio telescope technology, such as the development of larger and more sensitive arrays, can improve our ability to detect and analyze faint signals from distant civilizations.

    - Projects like the Square Kilometre Array (SKA) aim to create a powerful radio telescope array with unprecedented sensitivity and resolution.

2. **Optical Communication:**

    - Optical communication, using lasers or other directed light sources, offers the potential for faster and more efficient communication than traditional radio waves.

    - Laser-based communication systems could enable high-speed data transmission between star systems.

    - Advancements in laser technology, along with the development of sophisticated encoding and decoding techniques, are essential for realizing this possibility.

3. **Interstellar Probes and Autonomous Explorers:**

    - Sending interstellar probes or autonomous spacecraft to nearby star systems could provide opportunities for direct communication.

    - These probes could carry advanced communication systems and act as messengers, relaying information back to Earth or transmitting signals to potential extraterrestrial civilizations.

    - Developments in miniaturization, propulsion systems, and long-duration space travel will be vital for making interstellar missions a reality.

4. **Quantum Communication:**

    - Quantum communication leverages the principles of quantum mechanics to enable secure and instantaneous transmission of information.

    - Quantum entanglement and quantum key distribution techniques could revolutionize interstellar communication by providing secure and tamper-proof communication channels.

    - Ongoing research in quantum information science holds the potential for significant advancements in secure interstellar communication.

5. **Artificial Intelligence (AI):**

    - AI technologies can play a crucial role in processing and interpreting complex signals from potential extraterrestrial civilizations.

    - Machine learning algorithms can aid in deciphering unknown communication protocols and recognizing patterns that may indicate intelligent intent.

    - AI could enhance our ability to detect and analyze potential extraterrestrial signals, accelerating the search for communication.

6. **Future Possibilities:**

    - As technology continues to advance, future possibilities for interstellar communication may include novel approaches such as neutrino communication, gravitational wave communication, or even harnessing the power of quantum entanglement for instantaneous information transfer.

    - Additionally, breakthroughs in our understanding of fundamental physics and the nature of space-time could lead to revolutionary communication concepts that are currently beyond our imagination.

It is important to note that the technological challenges of interstellar communication are immense, and the successful realization of these future possibilities may require significant advancements in various fields. Collaboration between scientists, engineers, and researchers from different disciplines will be crucial in pushing the boundaries of interstellar communication and increasing our chances of establishing contact with extraterrestrial civilizations.

Implications and Consequences of Contact

Cultural, Societal, and Philosophical Ramifications

The potential contact with extraterrestrial life carries profound implications and consequences for our culture, society, and philosophical outlook. This entry explores some of the key considerations and potential ramifications:

1. **Cultural Impact:**

    - Contact with extraterrestrial civilizations can challenge our cultural beliefs, traditions, and worldviews.
    - It may prompt a reevaluation of our place in the universe, our understanding of intelligent life, and our concepts of identity, spirituality, and purpose.
    - Cultural exchanges with alien civilizations could lead to the enrichment and evolution of human culture through the sharing of knowledge, art, and ideas.

2. **Societal Transformations:**

    - Contact with extraterrestrial life has the potential to trigger significant societal transformations.
    - It may foster global cooperation and unity as humanity grapples with the realization that we are part of a broader cosmic community.
    - The challenges and opportunities presented by contact could lead to social, political, and economic changes as we navigate the complexities of interacting with advanced civilizations.

3. **Ethical and Moral Considerations:**

    - Contact with extraterrestrial life raises profound ethical and moral questions.
    - How should we approach the rights and autonomy of alien beings? How should we handle potential conflicts of interest or differing value systems?
    - Ethical frameworks may need to be developed or revised to guide our interactions and ensure fairness, respect, and the preservation of biodiversity and cultural diversity.

4. **Philosophical Paradigm Shifts:**
   - The discovery of extraterrestrial life can trigger paradigm shifts in our philosophical and scientific understanding of the universe.
   - It challenges our anthropocentric view and may require us to rethink concepts such as the nature of consciousness, intelligence, and the origin of life.
   - It could also provide insights into fundamental philosophical questions regarding the existence of other sentient beings, the nature of reality, and our place in the cosmic tapestry.

5. **Impact on Religion and Belief Systems:**
   - Contact with extraterrestrial life could have profound implications for religious and belief systems.
   - It may prompt theological and philosophical debates, requiring reinterpretation or recontextualization of religious texts and doctrines.
   - Some religious perspectives may embrace the existence of extraterrestrial life as part of a divine plan, while others may face challenges reconciling new discoveries with established beliefs.

6. **Scientific Advancements and Knowledge Expansion:**
   - Contact with extraterrestrial civilizations would provide an unprecedented opportunity for scientific advancements and the expansion of knowledge.
   - It could accelerate our understanding of biology, physics, astronomy, and other scientific disciplines through the exchange of information and collaboration.
   - Discoveries related to advanced technologies, alternative biochemistries, and societal structures could revolutionize our scientific paradigms and open up new avenues of exploration.

The implications and consequences of contact with extraterrestrial life are complex and multifaceted. They encompass cultural, societal, ethical, philosophical, and scientific dimensions. Preparing for such contact requires thoughtful consideration of these ramifications and the development of frameworks to navigate the challenges and embrace the potential benefits of engaging with intelligent civilizations beyond Earth.

Technological Impact on Humanity and Earth

Contact with extraterrestrial life has the potential to bring about significant technological advancements that could profoundly impact humanity and our planet. This entry explores some of the key considerations regarding the technological implications of such contact:

1. **Technological Advancement:**
    - Interaction with advanced extraterrestrial civilizations could expose us to technologies far beyond our current capabilities.
    - Knowledge sharing and collaboration may lead to breakthroughs in various fields, including energy, propulsion, communication, medicine, and materials science.
    - Advanced technologies acquired through contact could revolutionize industries, improve living standards, and address global challenges such as climate change and resource scarcity.

2. **Impact on Earth:**
    - Technological advancements resulting from contact may have far-reaching effects on Earth and its ecosystems.
    - New energy sources, transportation methods, and environmental technologies could mitigate the impact of human activities on the planet.
    - However, there is a need to carefully consider and manage the potential ecological and environmental consequences of introducing alien technologies to Earth.

3. **Societal Transformation:**
    - The introduction of advanced technologies from extraterrestrial sources may reshape society and its structures.
    - Automation, artificial intelligence, and other transformative technologies could impact employment, education, and social dynamics.
    - Preparing for these changes requires proactive planning, including considerations of equitable distribution of benefits and the potential for social disruption.

4. **Ethical and Security Concerns:**
    - The introduction of advanced technologies requires careful ethical considerations.
    - Assessing the risks and benefits of incorporating alien technologies into our society is crucial to ensure responsible use and avoid unintended consequences.
    - Security concerns related to the misuse or unintended consequences of advanced technologies must be addressed through robust governance frameworks.

5. **Space Exploration and Colonization:**

    - Contact with extraterrestrial civilizations may provide valuable insights and technologies for space exploration and colonization.

    - Advanced propulsion systems, life-support technologies, and resource utilization methods could enhance our ability to explore and settle other celestial bodies.

    - However, careful ethical and environmental considerations are necessary to ensure responsible and sustainable space exploration practices.

6. **Human Enhancement:**

    - Contact with advanced civilizations may expose us to technologies that enable human enhancement.

    - Genetic engineering, cognitive augmentation, and other advancements could enhance human capabilities and potentially redefine what it means to be human.

    - Ethical and philosophical discussions surrounding the responsible use and potential risks of human enhancement technologies become increasingly important.

The technological impact of contact with extraterrestrial life holds immense potential for progress and transformation. It necessitates careful consideration of the ethical, environmental, and societal implications to ensure that these advancements benefit humanity and our planet while minimizing potential risks and unintended consequences. Responsible and forward-thinking approaches are essential to navigate the transformative power of extraterrestrial technologies.

Protocols and Ethics in Interactions with Extraterrestrial Life

As humanity ventures further into the exploration and potential contact with extraterrestrial life, it becomes crucial to establish protocols and ethical guidelines for these interactions. This entry examines the considerations and frameworks surrounding protocols and ethics in our interactions with extraterrestrial life:

1. **Precautionary Approach:**

    - The precautionary principle suggests that until the nature and intentions of extraterrestrial life are better understood, interactions should proceed with caution.

    - Establishing protocols that prioritize the safety and well-being of both humanity and potential extraterrestrial lifeforms is paramount.

2. **International Cooperation:**
   - International collaboration is essential in developing protocols and ethical frameworks for interactions with extraterrestrial life.
   - Cooperation among nations ensures a unified approach, shared resources, and diverse perspectives in addressing the challenges and complexities of these interactions.

3. **Cultural Sensitivity:**
   - Recognizing and respecting potential cultural differences between humans and extraterrestrial civilizations is crucial.
   - Protocols should emphasize cultural sensitivity, promoting open-mindedness, and avoiding cultural imperialism in our interactions.

4. **Non-Interference and Prime Directive:**
   - The principle of non-interference suggests that we should avoid interfering with the natural development and evolution of extraterrestrial civilizations.
   - The concept of a "Prime Directive" advocates for non-interference in the internal affairs and evolution of less technologically advanced civilizations.

5. **Communication and Understanding:**
   - Establishing clear communication protocols is essential for understanding and interpreting extraterrestrial signals or interactions.
   - Efforts should be made to establish a common framework of communication, including the development of universal languages or symbolic systems.

6. **Ethical Treatment and Preservation:**
   - Respect for the intrinsic value of extraterrestrial lifeforms should guide our interactions.
   - Ethical considerations should prioritize non-exploitative practices, ensuring the preservation and protection of extraterrestrial ecosystems and lifeforms.

7. **Transparency and Information Sharing:**
   - Openness and transparency in sharing information about interactions with extraterrestrial life are crucial.
   - The scientific community, governments, and the public should have access to relevant data, findings, and deliberations to foster informed decision-making.

8. **Long-Term Monitoring and Assessment:**

    - Continuous monitoring and assessment of interactions with extraterrestrial life should be conducted to evaluate their impact and potential consequences.

    - Regular reviews of protocols and ethical frameworks are necessary to adapt to new discoveries, technologies, and societal changes.

Establishing protocols and ethical guidelines for interactions with extraterrestrial life is an ongoing process that requires interdisciplinary collaboration, international cooperation, and continuous evaluation. These protocols should prioritize safety, cultural sensitivity, non-interference, ethical treatment, transparency, and long-term assessment. By approaching these interactions with thoughtfulness and care, we can navigate the complexities and uncertainties while fostering a responsible and respectful relationship with potential extraterrestrial civilizations.

Alien Abductions and UFO Phenomena

Cultural and Psychological Aspects
Historical and Cultural Influences on Alien Abduction Claims

Alien abductions and UFO phenomena have captured the imagination of people around the world for decades. This entry explores the historical and cultural influences that have shaped the perception and

prevalence of alien abduction claims:

1. **Cultural Context:**

   - Different cultures have diverse beliefs, folklore, and mythologies that often incorporate encounters with otherworldly beings.

   - Historical accounts of encounters with celestial beings or entities can influence contemporary perceptions of alien abductions.

2. **Science Fiction and Popular Culture:**

   - The rise of science fiction literature, movies, and television shows featuring extraterrestrial life and abductions has influenced public perception.

   - Science fiction narratives, such as the Roswell incident, have become embedded in popular culture, fueling interest and speculation about alien abductions.

3. **Media Coverage and Sensationalism:**

   - Media plays a significant role in shaping public perception of alien abductions and UFO phenomena.

   - Sensationalistic reporting, documentaries, and fictionalized portrayals can contribute to the belief in and spread of abduction narratives.

4. **Psychological Factors:**

   - Psychological factors, such as suggestibility, false memories, and sleep-related phenomena, can contribute to the creation and belief in abduction experiences.

   - Cultural expectations, beliefs in supernatural or paranormal phenomena, and the power of suggestion can influence individuals' interpretation of their experiences.

5. **Social and Peer Influence:**

   - The influence of social networks, support groups, and online communities can contribute to the validation and reinforcement of abduction claims.

   - Peer interactions and shared experiences can shape individuals' beliefs and contribute to the formation of abduction narratives.

6. **Trauma and Coping Mechanisms:**
   - Some individuals who claim to have experienced alien abductions may have underlying psychological or traumatic experiences.
   - Alien abduction narratives can serve as coping mechanisms or attempts to make sense of distressing or unexplained events in their lives.

7. **Cultural Beliefs and Belief Systems:**
   - Belief systems, religious or spiritual beliefs, and the desire to find meaning in life can influence the interpretation of unusual experiences such as alien abductions.
   - Beliefs in the existence of extraterrestrial life and the idea that Earth is being visited by advanced civilizations contribute to the prevalence of abduction claims.

Understanding the historical and cultural influences on alien abduction claims is essential for examining their origins and significance. It is important to approach these claims with critical thinking, considering psychological factors, cultural contexts, and the impact of popular culture. Exploring these influences helps shed light on the complex interplay between human psychology, cultural beliefs, and the fascination with the unknown.

Psychosocial Explanations and Hypnotic Regression

When examining alien abduction claims, psychosocial explanations and the use of hypnotic regression have been employed to understand the psychological and social factors that contribute to the formation and recall of abduction experiences:

1. **False Memories and Suggestibility:**
   - Psychosocial explanations suggest that memories of alien abductions may be false or distorted.
   - Suggestibility refers to the susceptibility of individuals to accept and incorporate suggestions or leading questions into their memories.
   - Some researchers argue that alien abduction memories can be influenced by suggestive questioning, media influence, or cultural expectations.

2. **Hypnotic Regression and Recovered Memories:**
   - Hypnotic regression is a technique used to access and recall forgotten or repressed memories.
   - In the context of alien abduction claims, hypnotic regression has been utilized to recover memories of abduction experiences.
   - Critics argue that hypnotic regression can inadvertently create false memories or lead individuals to confabulate details based on suggestive cues from the hypnotist.

3. **Role of Media and Popular Culture:**
   - Media portrayals of alien abductions, along with books, movies, and television shows, can shape individuals' beliefs and expectations.
   - The influence of media can contribute to the formation of abduction narratives during hypnotic regression sessions.
   - Media exposure to abduction stories may prime individuals to interpret their experiences through the lens of alien abduction.

4. **Fantasy Proneness and Dissociation:**
   - Some individuals who claim to have experienced alien abductions may exhibit traits associated with high fantasy proneness.
   - Fantasy proneness refers to a person's tendency to have intense and vivid fantasy experiences.
   - Dissociation, a psychological process involving a detachment from one's thoughts, feelings, or surroundings, has been proposed as a potential factor in abduction experiences.

5. **Coping with Trauma and Anxiety:**
   - Psychosocial explanations posit that abduction narratives may serve as a coping mechanism for underlying psychological distress or trauma.
   - Abduction experiences could be a way for individuals to externalize or symbolize their distressing emotions or events.
   - The narrative of alien abduction may offer a sense of control or explanation for experiences that are otherwise difficult to comprehend.

It is important to approach the phenomenon of alien abductions with a critical and multidisciplinary perspective. Psychosocial explanations and the use of hypnotic regression provide insights into the complex interplay of psychological, sociocultural, and cognitive factors that contribute to the formation and recall of abduction experiences. By understanding these factors, researchers can gain a deeper understanding of the subjective nature of these claims and their implications for individuals and society.

Experiences and Narratives of Abductees

Within the realm of alien abduction phenomena, the experiences and narratives shared by individuals who claim to have been abducted play a significant role in shaping our understanding of this phenomenon. These experiences and narratives vary widely among abductees but often share certain commonalities:

1. **Encounter Descriptions:**
   - Abductees commonly report encounters with non-human entities, often described as extraterrestrial beings.

- These entities are frequently described as having distinct physical features, such as large eyes, slender bodies, and gray or greenish skin.
- Abductions are often said to occur during sleep or in secluded locations, with individuals recalling being taken against their will.

2. **Examination and Medical Procedures:**

    - Many abductees report undergoing various medical procedures during their alleged encounters.
    - These procedures often involve physical examinations, the insertion of objects or devices into the body, or the collection of bodily fluids or tissue samples.
    - Abductees frequently describe a sense of powerlessness and fear during these examinations.

3. **Missing Time and Disrupted Memories:**

    - One common aspect of abduction accounts is the experience of missing time.
    - Abductees often report periods of unexplained gaps in their memory during or after the alleged abduction event.
    - Memories of the abduction may emerge gradually over time, sometimes through spontaneous recollection or as a result of therapy or hypnotic regression.

4. **Emotional and Psychological Effects:**

    - Alien abduction experiences can have profound emotional and psychological effects on abductees.
    - Many individuals report feelings of fear, anxiety, confusion, and a sense of intrusion into their personal lives.
    - Some abductees may also experience ongoing psychological distress, such as post-traumatic stress symptoms or a sense of alienation from mainstream society.

5. **Similarity to Mythological and Folklore Motifs:**

    - The narratives of abductees often exhibit similarities to ancient myths, folklore, and cultural legends involving encounters with otherworldly beings.
    - Some researchers suggest that these similarities may reflect shared archetypal themes and universal human experiences that find expression through the abduction narrative.

It is important to approach the experiences and narratives of abductees with empathy and respect, recognizing that their subjective experiences hold personal significance to them. While the accounts of abductees cannot be easily corroborated or dismissed, they provide valuable insights into the complexities of human perception, memory, and the potential influence of cultural and psychological factors on abduction narratives.

UFO Sightings and Encounters

Notable UFO Sightings

Throughout history, there have been numerous notable UFO sightings that have captured public attention and sparked debates about the existence of extraterrestrial life. These sightings often involve unidentified flying objects or aerial phenomena that defy conventional explanations. Here are some of the most renowned cases:

1. **Roswell Incident (1947):**

   - The Roswell Incident is perhaps the most famous UFO case in history.
   - In July 1947, an alleged UFO crash occurred near Roswell, New Mexico.
   - The U.S. military initially claimed that it was a crashed weather balloon, but conspiracy theories emerged suggesting the recovery of an extraterrestrial spacecraft and the subsequent cover-up by the government.

2. **Phoenix Lights (1997):**

   - The Phoenix Lights refers to a series of UFO sightings that occurred over Phoenix, Arizona, in March 1997.
   - Thousands of witnesses reported seeing a large triangular or V-shaped craft with bright lights moving silently across the sky.
   - The event garnered significant media coverage and remains a subject of debate and speculation.

3. **Rendlesham Forest Incident (1980):**

   - The Rendlesham Forest Incident took place in December 1980 in Suffolk, England.
   - U.S. military personnel stationed at RAF Woodbridge reported encountering a series of strange lights in the forest, which they described as a UFO.
   - The incident is often referred to as Britain's Roswell and is considered one of the most compelling UFO cases in the country.

4. **Battle of Los Angeles (1942):**

    - During World War II, in February 1942, an unidentified object triggered a massive anti-aircraft artillery barrage over Los Angeles, California.

    - The incident, known as the Battle of Los Angeles, remains controversial, with some suggesting that it was an extraterrestrial craft or a false alarm due to wartime tensions.

5. **Belgian UFO Wave (1989-1990):**

    - The Belgian UFO Wave refers to a series of sightings that occurred in Belgium between November 1989 and April 1990.

    - Witnesses, including police officers and military personnel, reported seeing large, triangular-shaped objects with bright lights hovering silently in the sky.

    - The wave of sightings led to the establishment of a Belgian government UFO investigation group.

These notable cases represent just a fraction of the many UFO sightings reported worldwide. While skeptics often propose conventional explanations such as misidentified aircraft, natural phenomena, or hoaxes, these incidents have sparked ongoing debates and investigations into the nature and origin of unidentified aerial phenomena. The search for answers continues, as scientists, researchers, and enthusiasts strive to unravel the mysteries surrounding these intriguing sightings.

Military and Government Investigations

The phenomenon of UFO sightings and encounters has attracted the attention of military and government organizations around the world. In response to public interest and concerns regarding national security, several investigations have been conducted to examine these reports. Here are some notable military and government investigations related to UFOs:

1. **Project Blue Book (1952-1969):**

    - Project Blue Book was a series of systematic studies conducted by the United States Air Force to investigate UFO sightings.

    - The project, headquartered at Wright-Patterson Air Force Base, aimed to determine if UFOs posed any threat to national security and to scientifically analyze UFO reports.

    - Over the course of its existence, Project Blue Book collected and analyzed thousands of UFO cases, ultimately concluding that the majority could be explained by natural phenomena or human-made objects.

2. **Advanced Aerospace Threat Identification Program (AATIP):**

    - The Advanced Aerospace Threat Identification Program, also known as the AATIP, was a secretive program launched by the United States Department of Defense.

    - Operating from 2007 to 2012, its purpose was to investigate unidentified aerial phenomena with potential national security implications.

    - The program's existence was revealed to the public in 2017, and it was reported that AATIP had funded research into advanced propulsion systems and collected credible UFO sighting reports from military personnel.

3. **French Committee for In-Depth Studies (COMETA Report):**

    - The French Committee for In-Depth Studies, known as COMETA, was a private group composed of high-ranking military and civilian officials in France.

    - In 1999, the committee published a report on UFOs, titled "UFOs and Defense: What Should We Prepare For?"

    - The COMETA report acknowledged the existence of unidentified aerial phenomena and recommended further scientific research, improved reporting systems, and international cooperation in investigating the phenomenon.

4. **Chilean CEFAA Investigations:**

    - The Committee for the Study of Anomalous Aerial Phenomena (CEFAA) in Chile is a government organization tasked with investigating UFO sightings.

    - The CEFAA operates under the aegis of the Chilean Civil Aviation Authority and has conducted thorough investigations into numerous UFO cases.

    - In several instances, the CEFAA has released official reports on its findings, presenting evidence that remains unexplained and deserving of further analysis.

These military and government investigations demonstrate the recognition of UFO phenomena as a subject worthy of scientific inquiry and potential national security implications. While many investigations have yielded conventional explanations for sightings, some cases remain unsolved or continue to generate debate and speculation. The ongoing interest from military and government entities reflects the need for continued research and collaboration to better understand these phenomena.

Analysis of UFO Evidence: Photos, Videos, and Radar Data

When investigating UFO sightings, researchers often analyze various types of evidence, including photographs, videos, and radar data. These forms of evidence provide valuable information that can help determine the nature of the reported UFO event. Here are the main aspects involved in the analysis of UFO evidence:

1. **Photographic and Video Analysis:**

    - Experts scrutinize photographs and videos of UFO sightings to evaluate their authenticity and identify any possible explanations.

    - They assess the quality, clarity, and stability of the visual material to determine if it shows any identifiable objects or if it exhibits characteristics consistent with known natural or human-made phenomena.

    - Image enhancement techniques and forensic analysis may be employed to extract additional details or identify any signs of tampering or manipulation.

    - Comparison with known objects, landmarks, or celestial bodies can aid in determining the size, distance, and behavior of the observed object.

2. **Radar Data Examination:**

    - Radar data is an important source of information in UFO investigations, as it provides objective records of unidentified aerial objects.

    - Analysts examine radar returns to determine the object's flight path, speed, altitude, and any unusual maneuvering patterns.

    - They compare the radar data with other forms of evidence, such as eyewitness testimonies or visual recordings, to corroborate the observations and gather a comprehensive understanding of the event.

    - Doppler radar can also be used to assess any changes in the frequency of the radar signal, indicating the presence of a moving object.

3. **Scientific Methodology:**

    - Analysis of UFO evidence follows scientific principles, employing rigorous methodologies and logical reasoning to assess the data objectively.

    - Researchers consider alternative explanations and strive to eliminate known terrestrial objects, atmospheric phenomena, or equipment malfunctions before considering more extraordinary hypotheses.

    - Collaboration among experts in different fields, such as astronomy, meteorology, and physics, allows for a multidisciplinary approach in evaluating the evidence.

4. **Case Studies:**

    - Detailed case studies of well-documented UFO incidents provide insights into the analysis process and the challenges faced by investigators.

- These studies often include in-depth examination of multiple sources of evidence, including photographs, videos, eyewitness testimonies, and radar data.

- Through meticulous analysis and elimination of conventional explanations, investigators aim to identify any anomalous characteristics that defy conventional explanations.

The analysis of UFO evidence requires a careful and systematic approach to separate genuine unexplained phenomena from misidentifications, hoaxes, or misinterpretations. While many sightings can be attributed to known phenomena, some cases remain unexplained, intriguing researchers and fueling ongoing scientific inquiry into the nature of UFOs.

Critical Analysis and Explanations

Natural Phenomena Misidentified as UFOs

In the study of UFO phenomena, it is essential to consider natural phenomena that can be mistakenly identified as unidentified flying objects (UFOs). Many reported sightings have turned out to have plausible explanations rooted in natural occurrences. Here are some examples of natural phenomena commonly misidentified as UFOs:

1. **Atmospheric Phenomena:**
   Atmospheric conditions can create optical illusions, leading to UFO misidentifications. For instance:

   - Weather balloons, which are used for scientific research and data collection, can appear as spherical or elongated objects floating in the sky.

   - Atmospheric inversions, where temperature increases with altitude, can cause distant lights or aircraft to appear closer and exhibit unusual movements.

   - Lenticular clouds, which have distinct disk-like shapes, can create the illusion of flying saucers or structured objects.

   - Atmospheric reflections, such as sun dogs or light pillars, can create bright, elongated lights in the sky.

2. **Celestial Objects:**
   Celestial objects often cause confusion, especially when their appearance is unusual or unfamiliar to observers:

   - Planets, such as Venus or Mars, can appear as bright, stationary objects in the night sky, leading to mistaken UFO sightings.

   - Satellites, like the International Space Station (ISS), can reflect sunlight and appear as moving, luminous objects traversing the sky.

   - Meteors or bolides entering Earth's atmosphere can create brief but spectacular light shows, often misinterpreted as UFOs.

3. **Human-Made Objects and Activities:**
   Man-made objects and activities can also be mistaken for UFOs, particularly under certain circumstances:

   - Aircraft, including military aircraft, helicopters, or drones, can exhibit unconventional flight patterns or be seen at unusual times, leading to UFO reports.

   - Sky lanterns, released during celebrations or events, can appear as glowing orbs or lights drifting through the sky, generating UFO sightings.

   - Parachute flares used in military exercises can create bright, suspended lights that may be misinterpreted as unusual aerial objects.

4. **Perception and Cognitive Biases:**
   Human perception and cognitive biases play a significant role in UFO misidentifications:

   - Misinterpretation of distance and size: Objects at a great distance may appear larger or display unexpected movements, contributing to misperception.

   - Expectation and confirmation bias: Beliefs or preconceived notions about UFOs can influence how people interpret and recall their observations.

   - Group influence and mass hysteria: Collective experiences or shared beliefs can contribute to mass sightings and reinforce UFO narratives.

Understanding these natural phenomena and the potential for misidentification is crucial for critically analyzing UFO reports. Investigating UFO sightings requires thorough examination of all available evidence, including eyewitness testimonies, photographs, videos, and scientific data, to differentiate genuine unexplained events from misidentifications or hoaxes. By carefully considering natural explanations, researchers can separate the truly unidentified phenomena from those with rational explanations rooted in the natural world.

Psychological Explanations: Misperception and Illusions

Psychological factors play a significant role in shaping people's perceptions and experiences, including those related to UFO sightings and encounters. Misperception and illusions can contribute to the belief in extraterrestrial phenomena. Here are some psychological explanations commonly proposed to understand UFO-related experiences:

1. **Misperception of Common Objects:**

   - Everyday objects or phenomena can be misperceived as extraordinary or unfamiliar due to various factors, including lighting conditions, distance, and cognitive biases.

   - Examples include misperceiving aircraft lights, birds, kites, or balloons as unusual aerial objects with peculiar shapes or movements.

- The brain attempts to make sense of ambiguous or incomplete visual information, sometimes leading to misinterpretations.

2. **Optical Illusions:**

    - Optical illusions involve distortions or misinterpretations of visual stimuli, often influenced by the brain's attempts to impose order or patterns.

    - Certain atmospheric or lighting conditions can create visual illusions, making objects appear different from their actual characteristics.

    - For instance, autokinetic effect, where a stationary light appears to move when stared at for a prolonged period, can create the illusion of a moving object in the sky.

3. **Pareidolia:**

    - Pareidolia is a phenomenon in which the brain perceives meaningful patterns or faces in random or ambiguous stimuli.

    - When encountering indistinct visual stimuli, such as clouds, shadows, or rock formations, individuals may interpret them as recognizable objects or beings, including extraterrestrial entities.

4. **Sleep Paralysis and Hypnagogic/Hypnopompic Experiences:**

    - Sleep-related phenomena, such as sleep paralysis and hypnagogic/hypnopompic experiences, can contribute to perceived encounters with extraterrestrial beings.

    - Sleep paralysis is a temporary inability to move or speak while transitioning between sleep and wakefulness, often accompanied by hallucinations.

    - Hypnagogic experiences occur during the transition from wakefulness to sleep, and hypnopompic experiences occur during the transition from sleep to wakefulness. These states can involve vivid and immersive hallucinations.

It is essential to recognize that these psychological explanations do not discount or invalidate individuals' subjective experiences. They provide alternative perspectives for understanding the perceptual and cognitive processes involved in UFO-related encounters. Psychological factors can contribute to the formation of beliefs and narratives surrounding alien abductions and UFO sightings. However, it is crucial to conduct comprehensive investigations that consider both psychological and physical aspects before drawing conclusions about the nature of these experiences.

Extraterrestrial Hypotheses vs. Skepticism and Debunking

The debate surrounding UFO phenomena and the existence of extraterrestrial life often involves contrasting viewpoints between those who propose extraterrestrial hypotheses and skeptics who advocate for skepticism and debunking. Here are some key aspects to consider in this debate:

1. **Extraterrestrial Hypotheses:**

   - Extraterrestrial hypotheses propose that some UFO sightings and encounters are evidence of visitations by intelligent beings from other planets or civilizations.

   - Proponents of these hypotheses argue that the vastness of the universe, the abundance of potentially habitable planets, and the reported characteristics of UFOs suggest the presence of advanced extraterrestrial life forms.

   - They may cite eyewitness testimonies, alleged government documents, and unexplained physical evidence as support for their claims.

2. **Skepticism:**

   - Skepticism involves a critical and evidence-based approach that questions extraordinary claims, including those related to UFOs and extraterrestrial life.

   - Skeptics argue that the lack of compelling scientific evidence, the prevalence of misidentifications and hoaxes, and the limitations of eyewitness testimonies warrant a skeptical stance.

   - They emphasize the need for rigorous scientific investigation, empirical data, and adherence to established scientific principles before accepting extraordinary claims.

3. **Debunking:**

   - Debunking refers to the systematic examination and explanation of purported UFO sightings and encounters using scientific, rational, and logical means.

   - Debunkers aim to identify and expose natural or human-made explanations for reported phenomena, promoting a more mundane understanding of alleged extraterrestrial events.

   - They often highlight alternative explanations, such as misperception, hoaxes, conventional aircraft or atmospheric phenomena, and psychological factors, to challenge the extraterrestrial hypothesis.

4. **Scientific Method:**

   - Both extraterrestrial hypotheses and skepticism can be evaluated through the scientific method, which involves empirical observation, hypothesis testing, and peer review.

- Scientists and researchers strive to gather and analyze data objectively, scrutinize claims, and provide explanations based on the best available evidence.

- The scientific community generally demands robust and reproducible evidence before accepting extraordinary claims, including those related to extraterrestrial life.

The debate between extraterrestrial hypotheses and skepticism continues to stimulate scientific inquiry and public interest. It underscores the importance of maintaining a balanced and critical approach, fostering open-mindedness while subjecting claims to rigorous scrutiny. Only through continued investigation and the advancement of scientific knowledge can we gain deeper insights into the nature of UFO phenomena and the potential existence of extraterrestrial life.

Speculative Extraterrestrial Life Forms

Hypothetical Life Forms
Silicon-Based Life Forms and Their Characteristics

Silicon-based life forms are a fascinating concept in the realm of speculative extraterrestrial life. While life on Earth is primarily carbon-based, the possibility of life forms that utilize silicon instead of carbon as a foundational element has been contemplated. Here are some key characteristics and considerations related to silicon-based life forms:

1. **Silicon as a Building Block:**

   - Carbon and silicon share certain chemical similarities, as they both have four valence electrons, allowing for complex molecular structures.
   - Silicon-based life forms would likely require a stable environment with sufficient silicon availability, as silicon is less abundant than carbon in the universe.

2. **Alternative Biochemistry:**

   - Silicon-based life forms would have biochemistry that differs from carbon-based life forms, with silicon replacing carbon as the central element in their molecular structures.
   - Instead of carbon-carbon bonds, silicon-based life forms would likely rely on silicon-silicon bonds, which can form stable and complex structures.

3. **Solvent and Energy Sources:**

   - Water, which is a universal solvent for carbon-based life, may not be suitable for silicon-based life forms due to silicon's limited solubility in water.
   - Alternative solvents, such as liquid ammonia or hydrocarbons, have been proposed as potential environments for silicon-based life.
   - Silicon-based life forms may rely on different energy sources than their carbon-based counterparts. For example, they might utilize radiation or heat from volcanic activity as energy sources.

4. **Extreme Environments:**

   - Silicon-based life forms could potentially thrive in environments with extreme conditions, such as high temperatures or harsh chemical environments, where carbon-based life may struggle to survive.
   - The stability of silicon-based structures at higher temperatures and resistance to oxidation may make them better suited for extreme environments.

5. **Speculative Nature:**
    - It is important to note that the existence of silicon-based life forms is purely speculative at this point, as there is no direct evidence of their existence.
    - Theoretical studies and laboratory experiments have explored the possibilities of silicon-based biochemistry, but their feasibility and likelihood remain subjects of scientific debate.

While silicon-based life forms are an intriguing concept, further research and exploration are needed to determine their plausibility and potential existence in the universe. The study of alternative biochemistries broadens our understanding of the diverse possibilities for life beyond our carbon-based framework, stimulating our imagination and expanding the scope of astrobiology.

Gas Giants' Potential Floating Organisms

Gas giants, such as Jupiter and Saturn, present unique environments that raise the possibility of hypothetical floating organisms that could exist within their atmospheres. While the extreme conditions of these planets make it challenging for life as we know it to survive, the concept of floating organisms in the atmospheres of gas giants has captured the imagination of scientists and science fiction enthusiasts alike. Here are some key considerations regarding the potential for floating organisms on gas giants:

1. **Atmospheric Composition:**
    - Gas giants are predominantly composed of hydrogen and helium, with traces of other gases. The atmospheres of these planets are characterized by high pressures, strong winds, and extreme temperatures.
    - Floating organisms would need to adapt to these harsh conditions, potentially using specialized gas-filled structures or adaptations to harness the energy and resources available in the atmosphere.

2. **Aerostatic Adaptations:**
    - Floating organisms on gas giants may have evolved to maintain buoyancy and stability in the dense atmospheres. They could possess gas-filled sacs or structures that provide buoyancy, similar to the gas bladders of Earth's fish or the gas-filled chambers of certain marine invertebrates.
    - These organisms might also have specialized appendages or structures for propulsion or maneuvering through the turbulent atmospheric currents.

3. **Energy Sources:**
    - Due to the limited sunlight reaching the depths of a gas giant's atmosphere, photosynthesis would be unlikely as a primary energy source for floating organisms. Alternative energy sources, such as chemosynthesis

or harnessing energy from electrical discharges within the atmosphere, could potentially sustain these organisms.

4. **Nutrient Availability:**

    - Floating organisms would need to extract nutrients from the atmospheric gases or from other sources within the gas giant, potentially relying on chemical reactions or symbiotic relationships with other organisms.

5. **Adaptability and Evolution:**

    - The extreme and dynamic conditions of gas giants' atmospheres would require floating organisms to possess remarkable adaptability and the ability to withstand rapid changes in temperature, pressure, and atmospheric composition.

    - Evolutionary processes, driven by natural selection, would likely shape the characteristics and adaptations of these organisms over time.

It is important to note that the concept of floating organisms on gas giants is purely speculative, as no direct evidence of such organisms exists at present. However, studying the possibilities and constraints of life in extreme environments expands our understanding of the potential diversity of life forms and their adaptations in the universe. Continued exploration and advancements in astrobiology may shed light on the feasibility and existence of floating organisms on gas giants in the future.

Bioengineered and Synthetic Life Forms

In the realm of speculative extraterrestrial life forms, the concept of bioengineered and synthetic life forms extends the possibilities beyond natural evolution. These hypothetical life forms are the product of deliberate design and manipulation, either by advanced alien civilizations or potentially by future human technological advancements. Here are some key considerations regarding bioengineered and synthetic life forms:

1. **Design and Manipulation:**

    - Bioengineered and synthetic life forms are created through intentional design and manipulation of genetic material, molecular structures, and biological processes.

    - Genetic engineering techniques, such as gene editing and synthetic biology, could be used to construct life forms with specific traits, functionalities, or adaptations.

2. **Alternative Biochemistries:**

    - Bioengineered and synthetic life forms may explore alternative biochemistries beyond the carbon-based life forms that dominate Earth.

- These life forms could incorporate different molecular building blocks, alternative genetic codes, or utilize elements and compounds not typically associated with life as we know it.

3. **Functional Diversity:**
    - Bioengineered and synthetic life forms could be designed for specific purposes or environments, ranging from bioengineered organisms tailored for extraterrestrial colonization to synthetic organisms with specialized functions in scientific research or industrial applications.
    - The potential for customization and modification allows for a wide range of functional diversity among these life forms.

4. **Ethical and Philosophical Implications:**
    - The creation and existence of bioengineered and synthetic life forms raise profound ethical and philosophical questions, including considerations of responsibility, unintended consequences, and the blurring of the line between natural and artificial life.
    - Discussions around the ethical use and potential risks associated with the creation of these life forms are essential to guide responsible research and development.

5. **Existence and Detection:**
    - The existence of bioengineered and synthetic life forms in the universe remains speculative, as no direct evidence currently supports their presence.
    - Detecting these life forms, particularly if they incorporate alternative biochemistries or show signs of deliberate design, would require advanced scientific methods and technology.

It is crucial to recognize that bioengineered and synthetic life forms are speculative concepts rooted in scientific imagination and ongoing advancements in genetic engineering and synthetic biology. While we have yet to encounter or create such life forms, contemplating their possibilities broadens our understanding of the potential diversity and complexity of life in the universe and prompts important discussions regarding ethics, responsibility, and our place in the cosmos.

Alien Ecologies and Evolution

Adaptive Strategies in Extreme Environments

In the realm of speculative extraterrestrial life forms, the concept of alien ecologies and evolution explores the adaptations and strategies that life may have developed in extreme environments beyond Earth. These hypothetical life forms are envisioned to thrive in conditions that would be considered inhospitable or challenging for life as we know it. Here are some key considerations regarding adaptive strategies in extreme environments:

1. **Extreme Environments:**
   - Extreme environments refer to conditions such as high temperatures, low temperatures, high pressures, radiation, acidic or alkaline pH levels, and other challenging physical and chemical conditions.
   - Alien ecologies may have evolved specialized adaptations to withstand and thrive in these extreme environments.

2. **Extremophile Life Forms:**
   - Extremophile life forms on Earth provide insights into potential adaptive strategies in extreme environments. These organisms are capable of surviving and thriving in environments that are hostile to most life forms.
   - Hypothetical alien ecologies could harbor extremophile life forms that have developed unique biochemical processes, structural adaptations, and metabolic pathways to cope with extreme conditions.

3. **Biochemical Adaptations:**
   - Alien life forms may exhibit novel biochemical adaptations to survive in extreme environments.
   - These adaptations might involve the use of alternative solvents, such as liquid methane or ammonia, rather than water, as a medium for life processes.
   - Alien organisms might utilize different types of organic molecules or employ unique enzymatic systems that are tailored for extreme conditions.

4. **Energy Sources:**
   - In extreme environments where traditional energy sources are scarce, alien ecologies may have evolved alternative strategies to obtain energy.
   - These strategies might include harnessing energy from geothermal activity, chemical reactions, radiation, or utilizing unique metabolic pathways to extract energy from unconventional sources.

5. **Evolutionary Patterns:**
   - Alien ecologies would likely exhibit diverse evolutionary patterns, driven by environmental pressures and selective forces specific to their respective extreme environments.
   - Evolutionary processes might lead to the emergence of specialized organisms, symbiotic relationships, and complex ecological interactions, adapted to maximize survival and reproductive success.

Speculative discussions about alien ecologies and their adaptive strategies in extreme environments stimulate scientific curiosity and imagination. While we currently have limited knowledge of extraterrestrial life, contemplating these possibilities expands our understanding of the potential diversity and resilience of life forms beyond Earth. Future exploration and scientific advancements will further enhance our understanding of the possibilities for life in extreme environments throughout the universe.

Exoplanet Ecosystems and Food Chains

When considering the existence of extraterrestrial life, one intriguing aspect is the concept of exoplanet ecosystems and the formation of food chains. While our knowledge is limited to Earth's ecosystems, exploring the hypothetical ecosystems of exoplanets broadens our understanding of the potential diversity and complexity of life forms beyond our planet. Here are some key points to consider regarding exoplanet ecosystems and food chains:

1. **Exoplanet Habitability:**

    - Exoplanet habitability depends on various factors, including the presence of liquid water, suitable temperatures, and the availability of essential elements and compounds.

    - Habitability also takes into account the presence of energy sources that could sustain life processes.

2. **Primary Producers:**

    - In exoplanet ecosystems, primary producers would play a crucial role in energy acquisition and the formation of food chains.

    - These primary producers, analogous to plants on Earth, might utilize different energy sources such as sunlight, chemical reactions, or geothermal energy to convert inorganic compounds into organic matter through photosynthesis or other metabolic processes.

3. **Energy Flow:**

    - Exoplanet ecosystems would involve the flow of energy through food chains or food webs, similar to Earth's ecosystems.

    - Primary producers would be consumed by herbivores, which in turn would be consumed by carnivores or omnivores, forming a complex network of energy transfer.

4. **Trophic Levels:**

    - Exoplanet ecosystems might exhibit different trophic levels, representing different positions in the food chain.

    - Higher trophic levels would comprise organisms that consume lower trophic levels, leading to energy transfer and nutrient cycling within the ecosystem.

5. **Adaptations and Interactions:**
   - Organisms within exoplanet ecosystems would likely evolve various adaptations to survive and interact within their specific environments.
   - Predator-prey relationships, symbiotic interactions, and other ecological dynamics would shape the structure and stability of exoplanet food chains.

6. **Biotic and Abiotic Factors:**
   - Biotic factors, such as the presence of predators, competitors, and available resources, would influence the composition and dynamics of exoplanet ecosystems.
   - Abiotic factors, including climate, temperature, atmospheric composition, and geological processes, would also have a significant impact on the formation and functioning of these ecosystems.

7. **Ecological Resilience:**
   - Exoplanet ecosystems would possess varying degrees of resilience, indicating their ability to withstand disturbances or adapt to changes in environmental conditions.
   - Resilience would depend on the diversity of species, ecological interactions, and the capacity for adaptation and evolutionary responses.

Speculating about exoplanet ecosystems and food chains stimulates scientific inquiry and expands our perspective on the potential complexity of life beyond Earth. While we currently have limited observational data, future advancements in space exploration and telescopic technology will contribute to our understanding of the habitability and potential ecosystems of exoplanets.

Speculations on Alien Reproduction and Life Cycles

When contemplating extraterrestrial life forms, one intriguing aspect to explore is their potential methods of reproduction and life cycles. While we have a rich understanding of reproduction and life cycles on Earth, speculating about those of alien organisms opens up a realm of possibilities. Here are some speculative ideas regarding alien reproduction and life cycles:

1. **Reproduction Mechanisms:**
   - Aliens may employ diverse reproduction mechanisms that differ significantly from those observed on Earth.
   - Sexual reproduction, a common method on Earth, may not be universal. Aliens might employ asexual reproduction, self-fertilization, or other unique reproductive strategies yet to be discovered.

2. **Reproductive Structures:**
   - Alien life forms may possess specialized reproductive structures or organs tailored to their specific reproductive processes.
   - These structures might serve purposes such as gamete production, fertilization, or the incubation and protection of offspring.

3. **Life Cycle Variation:**
   - Alien life cycles may exhibit tremendous variation, depending on environmental conditions, evolutionary pressures, and biochemical constraints.
   - Some organisms might undergo simple life cycles with distinct stages, while others could have complex life cycles involving metamorphosis or transitions between different ecological niches.

4. **Reproductive Strategies:**
   - Aliens might employ unique reproductive strategies based on their ecological context and evolutionary adaptations.
   - Strategies could include synchronized reproduction events, reproductive dormancy, or reproductive efforts tied to specific environmental cues.

5. **Parental Care:**
   - Alien life forms may display diverse approaches to parental care, ranging from no parental involvement to highly developed caregiving behaviors.
   - Parental care could include protection, nourishment, teaching, or guidance of offspring, depending on the ecological and social dynamics of their environment.

6. **Genetic Variation and Evolution:**
   - Alien life forms may exhibit different mechanisms for generating genetic variation and facilitating evolutionary processes.
   - Genetic recombination, mutation rates, horizontal gene transfer, and other mechanisms could shape the genetic diversity and adaptability of alien populations.

7. **Life Span and Aging:**
   - Alien organisms might have life spans and aging processes distinct from those observed on Earth.
   - Some aliens could have significantly longer or shorter life spans, while others might exhibit negligible signs of aging or have mechanisms to repair and regenerate tissues throughout their lifetimes.

Speculations on alien reproduction and life cycles are highly speculative and imaginative, as our understanding is currently limited to life on Earth. Further exploration and discoveries in the field of astrobiology, along with the potential identification of extraterrestrial life, may provide valuable insights into the diversity of reproductive strategies and life cycles beyond our planet.

Creative Extrapolations
Science Fiction Depictions of Extraterrestrial Life

Science fiction has long captivated our imaginations with its vivid depictions of extraterrestrial life. Through books, films, and other media, science fiction writers and creators have explored a multitude of imaginative and often speculative concepts related to alien life forms. Here are some common themes and depictions found in science fiction:

1. **Humanoid Aliens:**

    - Many science fiction works portray extraterrestrial life forms as resembling humans in basic body structure, with two arms, two legs, and a head.

    - These humanoid aliens often possess varying physical features, such as different skin colors, body sizes, and facial characteristics, to signify their alien nature.

2. **Non-Humanoid Aliens:**

    - Science fiction also presents a wide array of non-humanoid alien species that defy conventional human form.

    - These aliens can take on various shapes, sizes, and structures, including tentacled beings, insectoid creatures, amorphous blobs, or energy-based life forms.

3. **Alien Intelligence:**

    - Science fiction explores a spectrum of alien intelligence levels, ranging from primitive or animal-like creatures to highly advanced and technologically superior beings.

    - Some works envision alien species with vastly superior intellectual capacities, telepathic abilities, or collective consciousness.

4. **Alien Civilizations:**

    - Science fiction often portrays complex alien civilizations with their own cultures, societies, and political systems.

    - These civilizations may have different modes of communication, social structures, and moral frameworks, providing a glimpse into alternative ways of organizing societies.

5. **Alien Biology and Physiology:**
    - Science fiction speculates on diverse alien biologies, with unique physiological traits and adaptations suited to their home planets.
    - These depictions include extreme environmental adaptations, unconventional sensory organs, symbiotic relationships, or exotic modes of respiration.

6. **Exotic Ecosystems:**
    - Science fiction explores imaginative extraterrestrial ecosystems, often showcasing the interplay between alien organisms and their environments.
    - These ecosystems might feature bizarre flora and fauna, exotic symbiotic relationships, or novel ecological dynamics.

7. **Alien Motivations and Agendas:**
    - Science fiction delves into the motivations and agendas of alien species, ranging from peaceful exploration and cooperation to conquest and domination.
    - These depictions often explore themes of interspecies conflicts, cultural clashes, and the potential for cooperation or coexistence.

Science fiction offers a canvas for creative extrapolations of extraterrestrial life, pushing the boundaries of our imagination and challenging our understanding of biology, intelligence, and social systems. While these depictions are often speculative and fictional, they inspire curiosity and encourage us to contemplate the vast possibilities that the universe may hold.

Imaginative Speculations and Alien Archetypes

In the realm of speculative extraterrestrial life, science fiction has given rise to various imaginative speculations and recurring alien archetypes. These archetypes, often rooted in cultural and historical influences, have shaped our collective perception of what alien life might be like. Here are some prominent examples:

1. **The Grey Aliens:**
    - The Grey alien archetype, popularized by accounts of alien abductions and encounters, portrays beings with slender bodies, large heads, and distinctive almond-shaped eyes.
    - These aliens are often depicted as technologically advanced, with a focus on scientific research and experimentation.

2. **The Reptilians:**
    - Reptilian aliens, also known as reptoids or lizard people, are frequently depicted in science fiction and conspiracy theories.

- These beings are characterized by reptile-like features, including scaly skin, snakelike eyes, and sometimes even the ability to shape-shift.
- They are often portrayed as powerful and secretive, influencing human societies from behind the scenes.

3. **The Insectoids:**
   - Insectoid aliens draw inspiration from the fascinating world of insects, featuring characteristics such as exoskeletons, multiple limbs, and compound eyes.
   - These aliens are often depicted as part of highly organized hive-like societies, with a strong emphasis on cooperation and specialization.

4. **The Energy Beings:**
   - Energy beings are ethereal and non-physical entities that exist in a state beyond conventional matter.
   - They are often portrayed as beings of pure energy, capable of manipulating and harnessing different forms of energy.
   - Energy beings may possess advanced knowledge and consciousness, existing in higher dimensions or alternate planes of existence.

5. **The Human-Hybrid Aliens:**
   - Human-hybrid aliens are depicted as a blend of human and extraterrestrial traits, often suggesting a connection or genetic manipulation between humans and alien species.
   - These aliens may possess enhanced abilities, psychic powers, or a unique blend of physical characteristics from both species.

6. **The Lovecraftian Horrors:**
   - Inspired by the works of H.P. Lovecraft, these aliens are often portrayed as cosmic entities beyond human comprehension.
   - Lovecraftian aliens are characterized by their vast size, tentacled appendages, and the ability to drive humans to madness by their mere presence.

7. **The Ancient Aliens:**
   - This archetype suggests that extraterrestrial beings visited Earth in ancient times, influencing human civilization and technological development.
   - Ancient alien depictions often involve gods, deities, or celestial beings with advanced knowledge and technologies.

These archetypes and imaginative speculations serve as creative frameworks for exploring the possibilities of extraterrestrial life. While they may not reflect the actual nature of alien life, they fuel our imagination and inspire new narratives, offering glimpses into the vast diversity of possibilities that the universe may hold.

Artistic Representations and Alien Aesthetics

Artistic representations of extraterrestrial life often play a significant role in shaping our visual perception of aliens. Artists and designers have used their creativity to imagine diverse and captivating alien aesthetics. Here are some key aspects of artistic representations of extraterrestrial life:

1. **Alien Physiology:**

    - Artists imagine a wide range of physical characteristics for alien beings, exploring unique body shapes, sizes, and proportions.
    - They may depict aliens with multiple limbs, non-humanoid body structures, or unconventional sensory organs.
    - Artists often employ vivid colors, intricate patterns, and imaginative textures to give the impression of alien biology.

2. **Otherworldly Features:**

    - Artists strive to create alien beings that appear truly "otherworldly" and distinct from terrestrial life.
    - This can involve the use of unconventional skin textures, bioluminescence, iridescent colors, or even incorporeal and ethereal forms.
    - The goal is to evoke a sense of wonder and unfamiliarity, highlighting the alien nature of these beings.

3. **Cultural Influences:**

    - Artistic representations of aliens are often influenced by cultural and mythological references.
    - Artists may draw inspiration from folklore, ancient legends, and cultural aesthetics to shape the visual appearance of alien races.
    - This approach allows for the creation of unique and evocative alien civilizations with their own symbolic meanings and visual narratives.

4. **Technology and Clothing:**

    - Artists often incorporate advanced technologies and futuristic clothing into their depictions of alien civilizations.
    - They imagine complex machinery, futuristic architecture, and sophisticated gadgets that reflect the technological prowess of alien societies.

- Alien attire may feature intricate designs, unusual materials, and symbolic elements that communicate the cultural values and social structures of these beings.

5. **Emotional Expression:**

    - Artists explore the portrayal of emotions and expressions in alien beings, considering how these non-human entities might convey their feelings.

    - This can involve the use of exaggerated facial features, body language, or abstract representations to communicate emotional states.

6. **Context and Environment:**

    - Artists consider the environment and context in which aliens exist, creating illustrations that depict their native planets, habitats, or spaceships.

    - They often pay attention to the interaction between alien life and their surroundings, showing how they adapt to different ecosystems and climates.

Artistic representations of extraterrestrial life offer a visual language that sparks our imagination and invites us to contemplate the diversity and wonder of the cosmos. These depictions not only entertain us but also broaden our perspectives on what life beyond Earth might look like. Through their creative interpretations, artists contribute to the ongoing exploration of the possibilities and mysteries of alien aesthetics.

Conclusion

In this book, we have embarked on a captivating journey through the realms of extraterrestrial life. From the exploration of our own solar system to the search for habitable exoplanets and the speculations about alternative biochemistries, we have delved into the fascinating possibilities that lie beyond our planet.

Through the chapters, we have examined the various theories and hypotheses about the origins of life, explored the conditions necessary for life to thrive, and investigated the potential for life to exist in extreme environments. We have also delved into the exciting field of astrobiology and its quest to unravel the mysteries of life beyond Earth.

We have witnessed the remarkable advancements in space exploration and the technologies that have enabled us to peer into the vast expanse of the universe. The missions, probes, and telescopes have expanded our knowledge and fueled our curiosity, bringing us closer to the possibility of discovering extraterrestrial life.

We have examined the challenges of interstellar communication and contemplated the implications and consequences of contact with intelligent civilizations. The cultural, societal, and philosophical ramifications of such encounters have provoked deep reflection on our place in the cosmos.

While investigating reports of alien abductions and UFO phenomena, we have encountered the complexities of human perception, the psychological explanations, and the ongoing debate between extraterrestrial hypotheses and skepticism.

Our exploration culminated in the realm of speculation, where we ventured into the realm of hypothetical life forms, alien ecologies, and imaginative representations. Through science fiction and artistic interpretations, we have embraced the creative side of our quest to understand and imagine extraterrestrial life.

As we conclude this journey, it is clear that the quest for extraterrestrial life is far from over. The search continues, fueled by scientific curiosity, technological advancements, and the human desire to unlock the mysteries of the universe. Each discovery, each piece of evidence, and each new question only deepens our fascination and compels us to explore further.

Whether we find microbial life on Mars, detect biosignatures on distant exoplanets, or make contact with intelligent civilizations, the implications for our understanding of life, our place in the cosmos, and the future of humanity are profound. It is a journey of discovery that unites us in our shared curiosity and reminds us of the vast possibilities that await us beyond our home planet.

As we turn the final page of this book, we are reminded that the search for extraterrestrial life is not only a scientific endeavor but also a deeply human one. It is a testament to our innate curiosity, our insatiable thirst for knowledge, and our profound longing to explore the unknown.

So, let us continue to gaze at the stars, push the boundaries of our understanding, and embrace the wondrous possibilities that await us in the vast cosmic ocean. The quest for extraterrestrial life is an eternal voyage, one that invites us to ponder the grandeur of the universe and our place within it.

May this book serve as a guide and inspiration as we embark on this extraordinary journey of discovery, exploration, and the pursuit of the unknown.

Disclaimer

This book serves as a comprehensive exploration of the topic of extraterrestrial life, combining research-based information with speculative concepts. It is important to note that while efforts have been made to provide accurate and up-to-date information, the content presented in this book may evolve over time as new scientific discoveries emerge.

The information contained herein is a compilation of existing knowledge, scientific theories, and hypotheses, as well as speculative ideas. The purpose is to provide readers with a comprehensive overview of the subject matter and to stimulate curiosity and imagination.

It is crucial to understand that the opinions expressed within this book, including any speculative or imaginative content, are not necessarily those of the author or the publisher. The book presents a range of perspectives, theories, and creative interpretations to provoke thought and discussion.

Readers are encouraged to engage critically with the material, conduct further research, and consult reputable scientific sources for the most current information. The content presented should not be taken as definitive or absolute, but rather as a reflection of the state of knowledge and understanding at the time of writing.

Furthermore, it is important to recognize that the field of extraterrestrial life and its exploration are dynamic and subject to ongoing scientific inquiry. New discoveries, advancements in technology, and evolving theories may lead to revisions and updates in our understanding of these topics.

The publisher and author disclaim any liability or responsibility for any inaccuracies, omissions, or misinterpretations that may arise from the use or reliance on the information presented in this book. Readers are solely responsible for their own interpretation and understanding of the content.

In summary, this book serves as a blend of researched information and speculative ideas, inviting readers to explore the possibilities and mysteries of extraterrestrial life. It is intended to stimulate curiosity, ignite the imagination, and foster a deeper appreciation for the wonders of the universe.